All the best as you optimize your strategy. Ron Price

Hope the book changes your future.

Create the Future You Want!!. Enos Brie

PRAISE FOR

OPTIMIZING STRATEGY FOR RESULTS

"It is not often one comes across any book that successfully combines principles, practices, and people. All three are required for success in any domain, and here the authors show how to effectively align them for results in an ever-changing world. A handbook for anyone who wants to develop and implement strategy that works."

—**Padraig Berry,** managing director, TTI Success Insights Ireland Limited

"*Optimizing Strategy for Results* is a terrifically written book that distills the complexity of organizational culture, strategy, and individual aspiration into a clear path of organizational success. Handling the new normal of volatile, uncertain, complex, and ambiguous (VUCA) environments takes a clear vision, set of values, and purpose. *Optimizing Strategy for Results* will be a wonderful thought partner that helps organizations navigate these uncharted times and environments we find ourselves in."

—**Ted Epperly,** MD, president and CEO, Family Medicine Residency of Idaho; past president and board chairman, American Academy of Family Physicians

"*Optimizing Strategy for Results* distills essential steps and a road map for the business strategy development process, expressed with clarity, inspiring and beautifully delineated complexity, to provoke a strategic mindset in illustratively cinematic terms. The authors brilliantly simplify strategy in precise, unsentimental prose for any category of business."

—**Dr. Charles Borura,** IT governance and strategy, Kenya Revenue Authority, Kenya

"*Optimizing Strategy for Results* offers a pragmatic approach to strategic management practice. It is one of its kind in Kenya and, indeed, globally. This is especially demonstrated in the tools incorporated in the book. It is a recommended reference book for strategic management practitioners whose intention is to be of real positive impact to the organizations they serve. This is irrespective of whether serving as corporate executives or as consultants."

—**Patrick Mutisya,** former Group CEO, Sovereign Group Ltd;
former CFO, Kenya Cooperative Creameries

"Thoughtful, precise, forthright, and helpful. The authors are able to get right at the issues that need attention. This new book proactively helps organizations with their strategic planning by providing clarity regardless of the complexity of the organizational context. In addition, the authors bring a rare combination of organizational culture and results being equally attainable. The cultural competencies and international experiences of the authors make this a must-read for strategic leadership."

—**Dr. Eric Forseth,** Holland Christian CEO/head of schools; past provost Dordt University, VP at Northwest Nazarene & Mount Vernon Nazarene University

"*Optimizing Strategy for Results* offers a thorough, analytical assessment of the process of strategic planning. This book is divided into three segments—preparation, creating strategy, and optimizing strategy—which allows a systematic approach for applying strategic planning in your organization. Each chapter ends with segments on taking action and key takeaways, which provides you with triggers to integrate these academic concepts into your planning process."

—**Dr. Lisa M. Aldisert,** executive advisor and author, Pharos Alliance

"It has been a most exciting and rewarding time reading *Optimizing Strategy for Results*. It is an excellent and timely piece coming at the high peak of a very unpredictable, volatile, and ambiguous business environment. It is spot-on, clear, innovative, and simple in illustrating this complex environment we refer to as VUCA. I found this book interesting, very easy to understand, and very relevant. This progressively encouraging book will be of great value to many; individuals, families, and leaders in SMEs (small to medium sized businesses), as well as big business in the private and public sectors. It is recommended for all libraries and for those who seek and pursue growth and business sustainability in both good and not-so-good times.

The authors recommendation for a "wirearchy," as well as the deployment of situational leaders comes as a correct and timely antidote for collapsing hierarchical systems in turbulent times. Optimization of the knowledge and skills, as well as the utilization of the tools provided in this book, will truly enliven any business."

—**Professor Peter M. F. Mbithi,** former vice chancellor,
University of Nairobi, Kenya

"What if things go wrong? Are we on the right path? Are you making the right choices and tradeoffs, and are you deliberately choosing to be different in development and execution of your strategy? If you often find yourself pondering over these questions then look no further. This three-part, seven stage book by Professor Timothy Waema, Ron Price, and Dr. Evans Baiya will equip you with a new way of not only working but also a new way of developing and executing a resilient strategy for your organization.

I have enjoyed reading this book, as it is practical. My favorite parts are on building strategic intelligence and building strategic partnerships. It's definitely my new guide."

—**Ms. Millicent Awiti,** strategy and change manager,
National Social Security Fund, Kenya

"Many of us naively think of strategy as a brilliant blueprint that can magically take us to the realization of a powerful vision. Little do we know of the dangers lurking in our path. Peter Drucker has made it common knowledge that culture could eat strategy for breakfast. Yet few strategists get behind the scenes and address cultural issues. In this book, the authors place due emphasis on communication—such an important element in culture building. By reiterating the importance of communicating the why, what, when, who, and how of strategy, they draw in the stakeholders, giving them clarity and drawing them into ownership of the execution plan, thus improving chances of success.

This book comes at a time when most organizations are desperate for answers on how to navigate a VUCA world. In this book, we begin to get answers tied into strategy. The authors acknowledge the need for agility and invite organizations to speed up their response by relying on competence-based teams rather than on hierarchy. They offer ways of accelerating response times by providing clarity around what strategic decisions need to be made, by whom, and by when.

I particularly like the fact that this book puts people upfront and center by pointing out the need to place people where they are best suited and by showing everyone in the organization how to be customer-centric—literally making them feel and visualize superior customer value and then go after it."

—**Dr. Vincent Ogutu,** vice-chancellor, Strathmore University, Kenya

"Well done for the effort and commitment to get this book out! It is always great to read a book done by friends and be refreshed. I am sure other readers will find the same excitement as me. This book addresses a gap in strategy on issues relating to the current environment of VUCA and beyond: the coming of Gen Z to the workplace; the era of alternative reality, fake news, and social media; the emergence of China and the Silk Road strategy; Covid and other health issues; and the emergence of Africa post-colonial and its young people in an era of broad bandwidth and the internet. This book is simple enough to lay readers and challenging enough to the discerning strategist."

—**Dr. Julius Kipngetich**

OPTIMIZING
STRATEGY
for
RESULTS

A STRUCTURED APPROACH TO MAKE
YOUR BUSINESS COME ALIVE

■ ▲ ●

Timothy Mwololo Waema, PhD
Ron Price
Evans Baiya, PhD

AN INC.
ORIGINAL

An Inc. Original
New York, New York
www.anincoriginal.com

This work is being published under the An Inc. Original imprint by an exclusive arrangement with Inc. Magazine. Inc. Magazine and the Inc. logo are registered trademarks of Mansueto Ventures, LLC. The An Inc. Original logo is a wholly owned trademark of Mansueto Ventures, LLC.

Distributed by Greenleaf Book Group

For ordering information or special discounts for bulk purchases, please contact Greenleaf Book Group at PO Box 91869, Austin, TX 78709, 512.891.6100.

Design and composition by Greenleaf Book Group and Kimberly Lance
Cover design by Greenleaf Book Group and Kimberly Lance
Cover image: iStock/Getty Images Plus/happyphoton

Publisher's Cataloging-in-Publication data is available.

Print ISBN: 978-1-7360283-8-4

eBook ISBN: 978-1-7360283-9-1

Part of the Tree Neutral® program, which offsets the number of trees consumed in the production and printing of this book by taking proactive steps, such as planting trees in direct proportion to the number of trees used: www.treeneutral.com

Printed in the United States of America on acid-free paper

21 22 23 24 25 26   10 9 8 7 6 5 4 3 2 1

First Edition

CONTENTS

FOREWORD

BY DR. JAMES MWANGI,
EQUITY GROUP MANAGING DIRECTOR AND CEO, CBS

I believe that great organizations are created through well-executed strategies.

This book helps break down strategy into practical phases: foundation, creation, and execution, with structured step-by-step methods in all processes. If these phases are done well, they contribute to not only growth but also to the sustainable growth of organizations. This is a framework worth following. It matches well with the story and growth of the Equity Group and why I believe that a well-defined and well-executed strategy has been a critical part of our success.

Great organizations must spend a lot of time developing their purpose, vision, and core values. In my experience, getting these elements right is one of the priorities for top leadership. One of the things that I have found in leading the Equity Group is the importance of ensuring that our purpose resonates with our customers—their wants and needs, as well as what they value. We have been successful as a bank by innovating our products and services to respond to the changing needs and wants of our customers, who are largely SMEs (small- to medium-sized enterprises), while remaining rooted in what they value: prosperity. I found my experience in this respect beautifully resonating with the content in the strategic foundation stage in this book.

In addition, this book brings out something that is dear to me, that the purpose must be shared with the business's stakeholders, especially its customers. I particularly liked the quote from Simon Sinek that ". . . customers don't buy the products and services you provide; they buy why you do it." Finally, I could not agree more with the authors that communicating purpose, vision, and core values inspires pride, a strong sense of ownership, and an emotional commitment to the organization.

Great organizations are prepared for the unexpected events across business lifecycle. In fact, every business must be prepared for volatility, uncertainty, complexity, and ambiguity (VUCA) and this must be reflected in the strategy. For us at Equity Group, we have incorporated this mindset in our strategy, and we continually align our operations teams to predict and plan for potential VUCA events. This allows us to respond expeditiously to opportunities and potential threats. I cannot emphasize the importance of making VUCA-readiness part of the leadership and culture experiences as leaders are ultimately responsible for creatively anticipating and responding to VUCA events with their teams through timely engagement, communication, and innovation. Leaders must also take advantage of VUCA to safeguard and strengthen customer relationships, which ultimately determines the success of the business. This has been our experience.

Strategic intelligence is the principal building block for strategy development. The book comprehensively covers both internal and external environmental analysis, with the authors being very generous with several practical tools. I found resonance with the authors' argument that the process of gathering strategic intelligence is an ongoing process, resulting in strategy being continually updated.

One of the things that struck me as important is the skills that people need to be effective in developing strategic intelligence: futuristic thinking, conceptual thinking, creativity, continuous learning, and customer focus skills. I feel that this is likely to be one the things that many business leaders do not often consider.

But the issue that impacted me the most is the strategic partnership grid. This is a tool to be used to build successful strategic partnerships with customers, competitors, suppliers or vendors, regulatory bodies, and other key stakeholders. The grid maps alignment of purpose on one axis and the diversity of perspectives or ideas, competencies, and networks on the other. This grid demonstrates that synergistic partnerships only happen when there is high diversity in perspectives, competencies, and networks of relationships brought into the partnership, and the parties are aligned in their purpose. With this simple grid, I could explain why certain partnerships are successful while others fail right from the beginning. This grid gives Equity Group a tool to use in partnership building. I am sure many business leaders will find it useful too.

Great organizations are ambitious and clearly use innovation to deliver growth strategy. In fact, I am of the mindset that you cannot deliver ambitious strategy without "out of box" and "new box" thinking. This is why creativity and innovation are so important to our business. I believe they are the two sides of the "growth coin". When we started the bank, we focused on the low-income and unbanked people in Kenya. These segments were large but unserved and regarded highly risky by multinational banks. We also focused on raising money locally. This took courage and different thinking and being very innovative. We focused on speed and access to grow our customer base with lots of problem solving along the way. Without innovation, it is impossible to deliver growth. And without clear strategy and innovation potential, efforts are wasted.

The execution section has several illustrated tools, in terms of canvases, scorecards and templates. Leaders and operational staff involved in strategy execution have a rich repertoire of tools to guide them in effectively implementing strategy and realizing planned results.

We in Equity Group are still pursing perfection in strategy, and this book will contribute greatly to our pursuit.

BY RICK STOTT, CEO, SUPERIOR FARMS

Optimizing Strategy for Results is a powerful book for those leaders that believe people are the key to their organization's success in a VUCA (volatile, uncertain, complex, and ambiguous) world. There has never been a time when leaders have experienced more disruption; thus, there has never been a more important time to effectively and efficiently use this strategic development model. There isn't a country, industry, or company that has not been impacted by the COVID VUCA event over the last year, and those organizations that optimized their strategies, which were embraced by their people, survived and many flourished— while others did not.

We, the readers, get the benefit of the authors' extensive international strategy experience accumulated over decades. Professor Tim, Ron, and Dr. Evans deliver a practical and compelling framework that is iterative at its core and is wrapped with the power of people. I have been fortunate to be counseled by two of the authors for many years and have a first-hand appreciation for their depth of knowledge on this topic. It is not only their knowledge but also their passion that comes through in the text. They state in the introduction, "We care deeply about helping leaders and organizations improve how they prepare for, create, and optimize strategy." This is not just a nice thought. They really do care deeply.

From the authors' perspective, strategy is not only about planning or creating forecast models. The steps outlined provide a framework to create a vision from which strategies are developed, which are owned and executed by the entire organization. The clarity of this framework is certainly important, but pay particular attention to the people aspect of the process. That is where the real passion and wisdom of the authors reside. That is where the real power of the strategy development principles resides.

The best leaders intuitively understand the value of this framework, but even the best leaders can use this book to refine their own strategy development process, as well as infuse these principles throughout their organization. Ultimately, every good leader's hope is that the strategies are developed in a collaborative process and are aligned with the values of the organization. This narrative provides distinct methods to develop the strategy in a way that elicits ownership of the process, the execution, and the outcomes.

There are nuggets of wisdom throughout the book that can be applied to not only strategy development, but also to a variety of other leadership disciplines. As an example, the Introduction and Part 1 (Preparation) are loaded with organizational discovery and development tools that are powerful by themselves. The first half of the book not only builds a foundation for strategy development but also provides a strong tutorial on culture discovery and transformation.

Part 2 (Creating Strategy) provides the structure and practical exercises to build dynamic strategies that will succeed in a VUCA world. Again, the focus is on the empowerment and engagement of people in the strategy development process. The authors' thesis is that if the suggested principles are properly applied, the organization will feel ownership of the strategies. If the organization feels the ownership, the probability of long-term success of the organization is more likely.

The authors have also provided readers with a variety of tools of execution. These tools are practical steps that can be applied to the conceptual strategies. This section is so full of practical ideas that a leader will have to sort through to determine which ones align with their leadership style.

The powerful principle of continual improvement is promoted in Part 3 (Optimizing Strategy). Again, the authors have done a wonderful job at applying great leadership principles to strategy execution. Of course, consistent with the rest of the book, this section focuses on people and how to effectuate organizational change in a VUCA world.

The depth of the content may seem daunting, but it does provide every leader with a path towards improvement. The authors are very adamant this is a continual journey with a continuous loop of preparation, creation, and optimization. The seven steps, combined with a constant communication feedback process, will strengthen any organization's strategic plan process and execution irrespective of how successful they currently are in optimizing strategy for results.

BY KRYSTA FOX,
strategist and change leader; founder and CEO, Changeosity; former CEO of the world's number 1 economic zone, DMCC (Dubai Multi Commodities Centre), UAE

It is an honor to be invited to write this for a book that I believe will significantly impact the way we approach strategic thinking and execution.

When I opened the pages of *Optimizing Strategy for Results*, I was compelled to start at the end. Immediately drawn to the latter stages of execution (5 to 7), I was thinking about the many instances of compelling strategies failing to fly. Execution is a discipline that requires a framework, and most leaders and employees simply don't have those tools, and as a result give up on their strategies before any real gains are achieved. It does not have to be that way. *Optimizing Strategy for Results* shows a new way for anyone who wants to do a much better job of being a strategic leader and creating high levels of team engagement.

This is the kind of book where you need to get out your pencil and start making notes!

I am a big fan of this book because it provides a road map for the pragmatist. The authors do not submit us to the regurgitation of theory and unnecessary word count, rather, they show us the way to develop and execute powerful strategy. This can only be successfully achieved by practitioners who have done it, failed a few (or more) times, and worked out the most effective method. It takes years of real, gritty experience to achieve what inks the pages of this impressive manual. I have had the immense pleasure and privilege of working with Prof. Tim on challenging strategy assignments so I know this to be true.

My career has enabled me to work with many different teams on new strategies and I have also captained global business transformation teams that have delivered exceptional results. As a change leader and, like many, a student at the 'school of hard knocks', I have discovered that the toughest part of strategy is keeping it alive every day, as you and your team lay the stonework on the road to your vision. Here finally is a strategy guidebook that divides its focus in the right measure between ideation and execution. As the authors so clearly explain, strategy is not an event, it is a process that can lead to winning results when it is approached in the right way.

I wonder, then, why is it that most strategy books fail to give more than a cursory nod toward the hardest part of achieving strategic outcomes—the road full of barricades, blocks and bumps—execution? In *Optimizing Strategy for Results* you will find gems that will totally change the way you strategize and think about value creation. This book will also show you how to use tried, trusted, and effective strategy tools like Porter's five forces, SWOT, balanced scorecard, GANTT, and SMART.

Simplicity is a word to which I continuously returned while reading *Optimizing Strategy for Results*. The authors make it simple to create and execute effective strategy. For example, the most successful business change projects in my career have leveraged partnerships to build value, and yet I have never encountered the powerful simplicity presented in the likes of the partnership grid. I will not be without it again.

The good news is that the authors also understand strategy design every bit as well as execution, and there is more gold to be found throughout *Optimizing Strategy for Results*. You will soon be scampering toward the four Cs, with your SLOC in hand, while asking insight-generating open questions. Seriously, though, making strategy fun and engaging is one of the best weapons in your arsenal. This book provides a powerful framework for creative collaboration. If you believe, as I do, that all the answers are in the room, then *Optimizing Strategy for Results* teaches you how to extract them.

If you've ever been part of the kind of futuristic, conceptual, persuasive thinking described in Stage 3, Creating Strategic Thinking, you will have experienced the thrill of the creative process. In contrast, it is deeply satisfying to execute a strategy knowing the hurdles that have been jumped or smashed through. That is where *Optimizing Strategy for Results* leads business leaders down a new path, and any leader of change is the better for reading this insightful manifesto.

To Tim, Ron, and Evans, your collaboration on this book will improve the strategic capability of everyone who reads it.

To the reader, devour this book, mark its pages, scribble in the margins, experiment, and you will have built a toolkit that multiplies your ability to optimize your strategy and deliver results.

PREFACE

Strategy is a complex, multifaceted, and fascinating blend of analysis, interpretation, judgment, and courage. The greatest strategies fulfill both organizational purposes and individual aspirations. As consultants in the areas of strategy, leadership, and innovation, we have often found that there are many people within the organizations we advise who are not fully aware of, or engaged in, the preparation, creation, and optimization of their organization's strategy. In these situations, the organization will inevitably achieve suboptimal performance.

Making these individuals aware of strategy and involving them in the strategy process is not enough. In order to achieve the greatest success, there needs to be a deeper partnership with employees, customers, suppliers, and strategic partners. These partnerships should recognize the infinite value of individuals and connect their values and aspirations into something that drives the organization forward in fulfilling its purpose for all stakeholders.

At times, the organization's strategy will inform the individual's aspirations, and, at other times, the individual's aspirations will inform the organization's strategy. Therefore, the individual and the organization need to align for world-class strategy development and execution.

We have created a step-by-step model for preparing, creating, and optimizing great strategy that is carried out in seven stages. Each stage in the strategy process provides deep insights into the concept of strategy. These stages are designed for those involved in the process to have an opportunity to influence both the pertinent processes and each other, which will contribute to strategy ownership and collaboration across the organization.

As shown in figure 1, communication is a common activity that is practically integrated in all the stages because strategy execution that produces extraordinary results stems from a greater alignment of individual actions, vision, and purpose with the organizational priorities, vision, and purpose. This alignment produces ownership of and a commitment to the strategy.

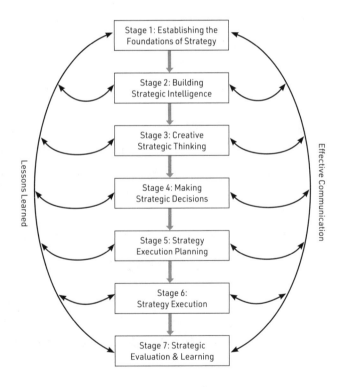

Figure 1. Stages of the strategy process.

The sequential nature of the stages is not fixed; we can move back and forth depending on the situation. For example, we can always return to the strategic intelligence stage (stage 2) whenever there is a significant change in the environment and modify aspects of the strategy in the specific stage we are considering. This flexibility is reflected in the feedback loop between the stages in figure 1.

In our conceptualization of strategy, we have infused new ideas and thinking from a number of areas that, to our knowledge, previous writers on the subject have not drawn on, making this book unique in its own right. The key areas we draw on are innovation, people first, axiology (value theory), and emotional intelligence.

For a combined total of close to 100 years, we have been engaged in learning how to develop and execute strategy as contributors, functional leaders, executives, and facilitators.

Prof. Tim, as we affectionately call him, has led strategy development and execution projects for more than 70 entities throughout Kenya, the Republic of Tanzania, and Sierra Leone. He was responsible for the first strategic plan ever created by senior management at the University of Nairobi and was a leading voice for its ongoing creation and execution of strategy for 15 years. During this time, the university grew dramatically and raised their status to become one of the top five universities in all of Africa. He has also been recognized for his work in developing national policy and sector-based strategy through several projects with governments in Kenya, the Republic of Tanzania, and Sierra Leone. Although he is a technology engineer through his postgraduate education, he has pursued his interest in strategy for several decades across all three sectors of business, government, and nongovernment institutions.

Ron first developed interest in strategy through entrepreneurism and his executive responsibilities for a variety of businesses. During his years as a leader for 10 different organizations, he was a student, bringing in the best strategy experts he could find to guide his leadership teams in the development of strategy. He began his consulting around strategy in support of not-for-profit entities during the 1980s and has led strategy initiatives over the past 30 years in more than 15 countries with both profit and nonprofit entities.

Dr. Evans, as we refer to him, has developed and executed strategy as a business leader and advisor in more than 20 different countries. As a result of his postgraduate studies in chemistry, electrical engineering, technology, and business management, he has integrated his expertise in innovation with optimizing strategy and increasing its dynamism for organizational performance. He has also developed a fierce conviction about the importance of aligning organizational strategy with individual aspirations. Dr. Evans often contributed to our discussions and writing as a contrarian voice, challenging us to rethink and expand our ideas about strategy and its practices.

We care deeply about helping leaders and organizations improve how they prepare for, create, and optimize strategy. We have written with the leader, facilitator, and passionate student of strategy in mind. More specifically, we believe this book will deliver valuable insights if you are a strategy practitioner who is not content with your current level of expertise. If you are convinced about the importance of creating and optimizing good strategy but frustrated with the current gaps between them in the organizations you serve, we hope this book will help you close the gaps. We also hope to reward your motivation to help others gain significant competence (and confidence) in the creation and optimization of good strategy and to master the creation, execution, and results of good strategy. We expect that you will connect with what we offer here if you are someone who is interested in advancing a robust framework with practical tools to become recognized as a world-class strategist and someone who believes that preparing for, creating, and optimizing strategy can and should be dynamic and fun.

Finally, we hope this book serves as an introduction for how we would like to help you on your journey of creating strategy for optimum results. We will continue to provide many additional resources, tools, case studies, and ideas on our website, https://strategyforresults. com. We look forward to learning more about your stories of creating strategy for results. Please send your questions, comments, and stories to info@strategyforresults.com.

INTRODUCTION

B efore laying the foundations for strategy, we address three specific reasons why mastering strategy is resisted, or minimized, in many organizations today. The first reason is because we are living in a constantly changing world that is evolving faster than ever before. Many leaders have opted for a more emergent approach that reflects reticence: Why should they develop a strategic plan when everything is changing so fast that the plan becomes obsolete within months of completion? This mindset encourages opportunism, often at the expense of much greater success over a longer period of time. We believe this is an erroneous approach that comes from not understanding the various stages of strategy and how dynamic and responsive they can be within a proven framework.

Second, many organizations give up on strategy because of cultural resistance to the discipline and continuous review or adaptations of plans. Too often, strategy is seen as something additional to day-to-day work. Instead, it needs to be embedded into the culture so that it integrates with day-to-day work and gives more relevance for long-term success. If strategy is the steering mechanism, then culture provides both the energy and power to make strategy happen. It is crucial to build a culture that is responsive, learning oriented, people oriented, and customercentric.

Finally, strategy often fails or underperforms because we don't recognize how aligning the diversities of people's talents, skills, and passions plays a key role in achieving superior results throughout the strategy continuum. As a result, assignments are often misaligned, resulting in confusion, mediocrity, and frustration. For too long, we have attempted to create and execute strategy without understanding the exponential possibilities inherent in discovering the unique contributions of a diverse group of individuals. This alignment requires that you understand and make use of the unique talents people bring to the strategy process and the skills that can be developed to optimize results in each stage.

STRATEGY IN A VUCA WORLD

Many companies are increasingly developing and executing strategy in a dynamic environment that has often been referred to as volatile, uncertain, complex, and ambiguous (VUCA). Without a doubt, how a business develops and executes a strategy may be complicated or made difficult by the environment in which it operates or intends to operate.

There is growing interest in the relevance—or lack thereof—of strategy in a world of constant change. Henry Mintzberg focused on this in his book *The Rise and Fall of Strategic Planning*. Because external realities change so quickly, many executives question whether going through something as comprehensive as the seven stages of strategy is a waste of time and resources.

One apparent fallacy of traditional strategic planning is the assumption that environments are predictable, and that strategy is only about vision and inspiration for the future. For many traditionalists, strategic planning has become an exercise of updating current plans and language to include broad goals, ambition, vision, and values. Each element is an important part of organizational life. However, they are often substituted for the hard work required to make good strategy that is contextual. They fail to identify challenges and make room for disorder, or to provide a coherent approach for dealing with those challenges. In fact, a good strategy must include the option to perform somewhere between good and great, despite the environment.

In the VUCA world, decisions are made with a clear understanding that "information no longer has prognostic value, because framework conditions change very quickly, coalitions of interests become more and more complex, and motives are constantly changing."[1] In VUCA contexts, established leadership, hierarchies, and strategies are all within the reach of disruption. If the organization is to survive, its leadership style and strategies have to constantly change. In VUCA contexts, the past experiences, dogmas, and established paradigms all become subjective. New thinking, flexible ideas, and new micro- and macrocultures are required.

VUCA tests even the best of organizations, and winning must be hard-fought. Unfortunately, VUCA can be a death sentence for many companies; they get drowned by the volatility, complexity, and sheer number of changes. Most of these companies have ambitious strategies that lack a detailed approach to reacting to different specific contexts, and many never get to create such strategies or have a saving branch to hold on to to keep from drowning. The good news about VUCA is that it disrupts everyone and everything, which affords organizations the opportunity to reestablish and execute differently and creatively. Other companies thrive in this disruption; they see VUCA as an opportunity to execute their detailed plans. They are swimming in VUCA instead of drowning.

HOW TO SURVIVE

Of course, everyone wants to be VUCA-ready, to survive, or—better yet—to thrive during disruption. This cannot be an accidental happenstance; it must be intentional. An organization takes a great amount of time and effort to fight changes, especially if it was not prepared. It can easily become overwhelmed, forcing people to make reactive and often short-lived bad decisions. In some cases, the organization becomes paralyzed and does not make opportunity-saving or opportunity-grabbing decisions. The organization has to spend additional resources to retrain and reshape its employees, which can also lead to the cancellation of long-term projects with more focus on short-term operational developments. In an unprepared organization, the two key areas that suffer most due to VUCA are organization culture and focus on innovation.

To avoid this reaction to VUCA, your organization must act. You need new thinking. Embrace change, make better decisions faster, evolve your organizational mindsets, and be focused on the future.

New thinking

When confronted with sudden change or ambiguous situations, most people overreact; they tend to want to make decisions quickly, to escape. In fact, most people rely on past experience or an emotional reaction to make a decision. If your house were on fire, would you run into the fire to try to salvage your goods without a plan? Probably not. But this is what companies do when confronted with volatility.

Let's say your organization is notified by a critical customer that they are considering changing suppliers because a competitor has given them the same product or service for 30 percent less. Typically, your team would panic, driven by the desire to respond to the communication right away. Hurried responses to the customer—without proper engagement with data, internal collaborators, or customer teams—are often an overreaction. This potential business loss, if thought through creatively, can be a great opportunity to not only keep the customer but also to improve customer value to the business.

The most common big mistake made is businesses using traditional "easy routes" based on education and data to react to volatility. For example, price discounting; driving for cheaper, faster, lower expenses; and pushing for more efficiencies. Although these reactions may be good, they are often suboptimal. Your business may survive the first event, but these tactics will not enable survival when you are faced with multiple events at the same time. Instead, you must think differently and broadly and act intentionally and quickly when faced with disruptive environments; you need a strategy for results.

Hierarchy versus wirearchy

During times of stability, every organization builds its culture, which typically involves a hierarchy determined by position and decision-making. When VUCA hits, to respond effectively and quickly, the hierarchy needs to be broken. Agile and situational leaders should emerge; this is called a "wirearchy." Organizations that do not welcome agility and allow people to emerge as situational leaders always stall—and often drown. To survive a VUCA environment, you must distribute decision-making and power across your teams so they think and act effectively and quickly.

Embrace change

Disruptive environments typically force change. Those who see the change for what it is wear their life jackets and start working in the next context to swim instead of flail. Those who resist change and embrace hope strategies drown. The organization needs to identify change, remove change killers, and equip its stakeholders to embrace and work in the new environment.

Make better decisions faster

It should be clear to all in the organization that everyone is responsible for some decisions. To help everyone make the right decision in a timely way, your team should be ready to answer these questions, at any level:

- What is the decision to be made?
- Who is the right person to make this decision?
- What is the ideal time frame for making this decision?

This won't ensure perfect decisions, but it will lead to better decisions over time. An entire organization of decision-makers will become a learning organization, and this increased capacity for better decision-making will become a strong competitive advantage in the creation and optimization of strategy.

As your organization learns to make better, more timely decisions, it will gain the flexibility to adapt more quickly to changing circumstances, have an increased awareness of emerging opportunities and challenges, and have a greater capacity for leveraging both strategy and agility in the VUCA world.

Evolve mindsets

When confronted with a significant VUCA event, personal and organization mindsets separate the casualties, survivors, and growers. In his book *Antifragile: Things That Gain from Disorder*, Nassim Taleb[2] introduces VUCA as a wind that can either extinguish or energize an organization.

Most VUCA events leave a permanent imprint on the organization. Therefore, it matters how you see change; if the organization is hoping that the change will go away, it typically becomes a casualty of the change, especially if it adjusts too late or never adjusts. If the company adjusts but with no intention of making a permanent change, it will likely survive—for a time. If the company embraces the VUCA event and sees it as an opportunity to create more value for its stakeholders, it will not only survive, but it will also start growing at the end of the VUCA event.

VUCA helps distinguish fragile, robust, and strong companies. Your organization must evolve the right mindset to deal with a VUCA event, otherwise it will be extinguished instead of energized.

Be future focused

People who have clear dreams of the future are able to withstand hardships longer and emerge healthier than those who do not. The same is true for companies. When going through a VUCA event, planning and thinking about the future beyond the event will also motivate the organization and its stakeholders to invest in winning while the event is taking place. In this way, they both can experience better times ahead, even if the timing may not be clear. Typically, the best mindset is *"the future is now."* This allows everyone to own and contribute to the present. Without an anticipated future—a vision—based in smart approaches and detailed plans, the stakeholders become apathetic and the organization eventually goes into triage mode.

THE ROLE OF STRATEGY

Strategy is the detailed game plan of how you are going to play and win in VUCA environments. This strategy must be simple, have a clear connection to customer value, and include clear decision-making criteria. It requires simple and actionable measurements and needs a consistent rhythm of reporting and communication. It must allow for agility and emergent thoughts. A simple strategy allows you to show its results openly and transparently so everyone knows how the business is performing against its objectives. It can point out any potential dangers. It will also show your strategy's success and everyone's part in it.

In *Great by Choice*,[3] Jim Collins and Morten Hansen describe empirical creativity as one of three core behaviors of what they refer to as "10Xers," companies that outperform their competition in the long term. Specifically, they argue that in situations of instability, uncertainty, and rapid change, companies should carry out empirical validation of whether a certain decision or strategic option will work. This is in contrast to reliance on pure analysis.

In a VUCA environment, strategy development and strategy execution are not separate; they are intertwined. Once strategic decisions are made to deal with a disruptive event, they are executed and continuously evaluated to gauge what the organization is learning from this execution—what works and what does not. The adoption of this learning perspective on strategy introduces flexibility, adaptability, and evolution. Simultaneous, continual tracking of the trends in the immediate and wider environment will give the organization's managers and leaders an opportunity to modify their execution of strategy and, indeed, the strategy itself.

CREATING A RESILIENT STRATEGY

A VUCA-ready strategy is detailed and anticipates changes in the key areas of the business. The strategy is informed partly by external assessment and partly by the organization's ability to adapt to external changes. This fulfills a basic requirement of a good strategy, which is to have a built-in, accurate view of what the organization is capable of controlling (externally) and what it is able to adapt to (internally). Of course, what the organization can control and adapt to changes from time to time, so the strategy must be evaluated continuously to match its context.

Anticipation

A company's strategy is often assumed to be good until it does not work. One of the reasons it can become ineffective is a lack of foresight for volatile conditions. Unfortunately, good strategies are rare, especially since most are built on ambition and hope. In fact, most "ambitious" strategies do not live up to the organization's expectations because they are built on shallow assumptions and not on deeply-thought-out scenarios. Therefore, if and when the conditions change, which is often the norm, the strategy fails.

Unfortunately, many companies have been victims of ambition-based strategy.[4] The recent global coronavirus pandemic is a key example. Responses to COVID-19 varied greatly around the world, with a clear contrast in the strategies implemented. The United States employed an ambitious strategy of hope-and-see, whereas Germany, New Zealand, China, and other countries embraced a deliverable approach to problem-solving, with clear goals, guidelines, and communication. The large number of deaths in the United States could be attributed to bad strategy, as could some of the closed doors of countless businesses.

Hoping a challenge will go away or blaming someone else is rarely effective, but ignoring a problem clearly visible on the horizon is reckless and irresponsible. The global health community had been warning about a global pandemic for years, and we'd even had precursors like bird and swine flu. Most businesses had no way to curb or avoid the pandemic itself, but they would have had the opportunity to reduce their economic losses—or at least to avoid decimation—if they had employed the right strategies before and during the crisis to navigate the situation. Organizations must be prepared for ever-changing conditions, which are then reflected in good strategy.

External assessment

One of the great benefits of a VUCA-ready strategy is organizational awareness based on an evaluation of the external environments that have the potential to significantly affect the organization's future. This assessment of external factors helps the organization understand its options if and when a disruptive event affects its future. To create the right strategy, the organization needs to be self-aware and evaluate its options and the level of predictability of those options. These relationships can be complex, but they will help your organization identify how fragile it is and where it can invest to survive.

There are four potential futures of an organization[5], as shown in figure 2:

- A truly uncertain future

- Unpredictable but varied futures

- Predictable but limited alternative futures

- A clear future

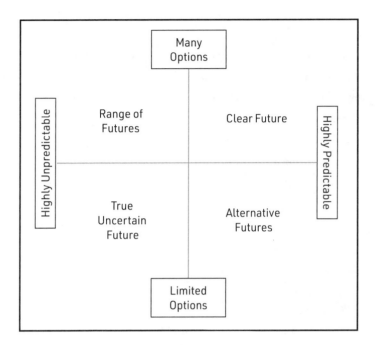

Figure 2. Potential futures.

In a truly uncertain future, the organization has limited options to pursue in the face of a VUCA event, and the predictability of its outcomes is low. Therefore, the organization is at the mercy of the disrupting event. The organization's strategy is unclear or based only on the circumstances when the strategy was created. This situation can occur if the organization has a significant number of external uncertainties, such as technology, demand, supply chain, and markets. The pandemic, for example, affected almost all parts of every business environment.

With a range of futures, the organization has many options, but its outcomes are still highly unpredictable. In the case of a VUCA event, however, despite the seeming chaos, you can choose what kind of future you want for your organization because of the many options. Multiple elements of strategy could drive toward one of the futures. For example, winning in a new market.

Alternative predictable futures allow the organization a high level of predictable outcomes, despite their limited number. Similar to the previous case, the organization can choose the kind of future it wants to have when a disruption occurs because of the high predictability, even if they have fewer options. For example, reacting to what a competitor may do in an oligopoly market.

When the future is clear, a strategy may not be needed. With many options and highly predictable outcomes, simple operation practices of precise prediction, such as market research, Michael Porter's five-forces framework,[6] and value chain analysis, will be enough to keep your business healthy. For example, a mature company with a stable supply chain and market needs no formal strategy to continue during nondisruptive times.

The kind of future the organization expects will dictate the types of strategy it should adopt in normal times. However, during VUCA times, the more uncertain the future, the higher the likelihood that the organization will be extinguished. This is true unless you have high organizational capability and adaptability to respond as part of your readiness for disruption.

Internal assessment

An internal assessment compares potential changes with your organizational capacity and how it responds to them. It helps build clarity and transparency in the organization and reveals what it is not ready for. This leads to better decision-making and the development of risk management measures, especially when the organization is not ready for or incapable of responding to certain changes.

An internal assessment will clarify your organization's strategic clarity and strategic agility levels, the alignment of its values with its readiness levels, its long-term commitment to growth and survival, and your leadership's ability to always be prepared. The goal is not to condemn those who find themselves in a poor status; it's to help them identify gaps that could be detrimental to the organization if they aren't addressed. It also serves to match the internal capabilities with the external contexts. The assessment serves as a guide when creating detailed, actionable, micro- and macrostrategies.

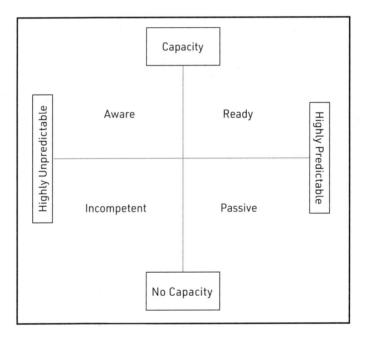

Figure 3. VUCA readiness assessment.

There are four levels of internal organizational readiness:

- Incompetent
- Aware
- Passive
- Ready

An incompetent organization is oblivious, placing itself in the most vulnerable position. The organization lacks knowledge of how to evaluate the use of its resources and has not organized those resources in readiness for any external change. This kind of organization is living in the proverbial bubble, where change does not exist. This is not reality, and the business is likely to fold under pressure.

If the organization is aware of potential VUCA events and has organized its resources for response accordingly, its outlook will be improved. However, in this category, there is no way to predict what the changes could be. This kind of organization either ignores the data or is apathetic to the changes, hoping they will not occur.

A passive organization is cognizant about the potential VUCA events and is ready for them, but it has not organized its resources to respond to such events. This kind of organization is often too busy with internal operations, prohibiting it from prioritizing readiness for potential disruptors.

An organization that is truly ready for disruption has organized itself to respond and has updated its predictions of potential VUCA events. This kind of organization has a disciplined and dynamic approach to the synthesis of data and risk management.

First, the strategy team must ensure that gaps are closed in its organization's readiness for disruption. After identifying the various VUCA vulnerabilities and putting them in the strategy as breaches to be closed, the next challenge for most companies is actually doing the work of closing them. One mistake that companies make is having individual teams work on strategic gaps. When individual teams work on gaps, they're never closed quickly or in the right level of detail. The organization-wide strategy must include gaps with their closure adopted as the goal of every stakeholder. Your company can quickly close VUCA gaps through innovation and coordination.

Whenever a VUCA gap is identified, the organization should move with speed to address it. This requires a different mindset that incorporates agility, pivots, and distributed decision-making. Further, you must address a perceived gap at the same speed you would if the VUCA had already arrived. This calls for competence-based teams instead of a hierarchy. The organization should find the most competent people in various subject areas, create teams based on individual skill sets, and mandate them to create solutions that are both valuable and scalable. Innovation is a VUCA-ready best friend and ultimate antidote during disruption.

BUILDING AN ALIGNED CULTURE

A company's organizational leadership is ultimately responsible for its results and welfare. It takes anticipatory leadership to be ready for VUCA events. Leaders in the organization must prepare for the future—in the short, medium, and long term. Preparedness is not only reflected in the strategy but also in the organizational vision; its paradigms of understanding, clarity, adaptability, agility, and decision-making; its values; and its culture. As a leader, you must also engage as many people as possible in the strategy development process at as many different levels as possible. Strategy development is a creative process that needs people's capacity to generate rational questions and answers, as well as intuition and wisdom.[7]

Jim Collins and Morten Hansen argue in *Great by Choice* that an environment of chaos and uncertainty does not determine why some companies thrive and why others don't; people do. For example, people provide leadership under such circumstances, people come up with creative ways to deal with the environment, and people pursue a purpose and achieve audacious goals and vision. If there is any element of luck, it is the luck of having the right people as leaders, managers, team members, and mentors. Organizations that are VUCA-ready have a healthy culture that is responsive, that is focused on learning, that puts people first, and that is centered on its customers.

Responsive culture

Responsive culture is built on the principles of fast decision-making, creating a capacity to retool and pivot, and a constant alignment with the market and internal stakeholders. Information is always treated not just as mere knowledge but also as part of a larger puzzle that must be understood and reacted to in order to be better prepared. The organization knows how easy it is to accelerate, to change direction, or to stop on any opportunities that arise. There is a deep understanding that, although the future in itself is a risk, a lack of preparation makes that future even riskier.

Learning culture

Learning culture is built on the principles of experimentation, execution excellence, and data transparency. Although normal business operations must take place, an organization with a learning culture is continually experimenting with ideas that will add value to its various stakeholders. It is not the size of the experiment that matters; it is the number of experiments, the outcomes, and the quality of gained insights. In this organization, learning is continual and eventually incorporated into daily operations, making it more efficient and always on the cutting edge. In a learning culture, continuous adaption and renewal of processes and structures takes place within the organization.

People-first culture

People-first culture is built on the assertion of understanding the organization's people. It places them in the best positions for maximum performance. Only the best-placed individuals and coordinated teams survive disruption. If the individuals are not well placed in the organization, they will tend to be disengaged. They may be the right talent in the wrong place. During a VUCA event, such individuals tend to drag the rest of the team down. That misalignment of talent and function also tends to make them unhappy; they often leave the organization when their expertise and knowledge are needed the most.

To create a people-first culture, you need deep knowledge about each individual. What are their talents and skills? What drives them? What is their level of emotional intelligence and thought processes? Such knowledge is critical in high-performing teams, especially under stress. During disruption, every organization needs its own special forces—a team of perfectly aligned talent and purpose—to address the threat effectively.

Additionally, when organizational and individual values align, the result is a synergistic relationship with the organization's purpose and meaning. The organization encourages individual autonomy and collaboration among team members, which increases trust and freedom and results in individual circles of control and collaboration that are much larger than their circle of concern.[8]

In a people-first culture, character and expertise are recognized to be higher than organizational position. Respect and recognition are paramount. Those who exhibit a willingness to learn and improve are encouraged to contribute.

A people-first culture appreciates, embraces, and sustains inter-generational and diverse teams. This is not just healthy for the team; it also gives the organization wider and more informed perspectives on how to deal with multigenerational, diverse customers. In a people-first culture, there is diversity in people, views, and passions, which, when aligned with a common purpose, leads to a healthier, more caring, innovative, profitable, and resilient organization.

Customercentric culture

Customercentric culture is obsessed with doing what is of most value to the customer. A customer-value mindset is embedded across all parts of the organization. Everyone in the organization understands how their job contributes to customer value and, eventually, to company performance. Everyone in the organization knows their customer, their customer's needs and wants, and what superior customer value looks like. Everyone understands how to respond to their customer when conditions change. Your leadership must invest in aligning talent, jobs, and customer value with individual performance. People-first organizations tend to be better customercentric organizations.

Everything rises and falls by the organization's leadership. This holds true with strategy. Organizational strategy is a direct expression of its leadership, which must guide with a great sense of agility and constant mutation to thrive. However, to lead the organization through the process of creating and being ready for disruptive change, the leader must have strong conviction to the purpose of the organization; have a strong sense of urgency; and have highly developed futuristic thinking, decision-making, problem-solving, creativity, and conceptual thinking skills.[9]

ALIGNING TALENT AND SKILLS WITH STRATEGY

After decades of helping organizations create, plan, and optimize strategy, we are convinced that the journey to becoming a world-class strategist must be customized to each person's unique talents, skills, and passions. Quite often, strategy is only considered through the prisms of process and structure, without recognizing the unique traits each individual brings to the strategy continuum.

In practical terms, all leaders have the ability to think creatively. However, not all leaders have equal capacities for creative thinking. For many years, we have used a battery of psychometric instruments to explore ways of measuring different degrees and styles of creativity. Some people are high-production idea factories, generating more than they could ever possibly implement. Others create new ideas with deliberation, often with more caution and concern about implementation. These people are often better at evaluating and sorting ideas than creating them. This is a much-needed component in the proper management and advancement of ideas.

For strategy that produces results, we need a broad spectrum of idea managers, from generating to evaluating, planning, implementing, and learning. Because these various aspects of idea management will be approached by strategists differently, the "secret sauce" to a successful organizational strategy is the ability to recognize and engage strategists according to the stages in which they can make optimal contributions.

In the same way, some people have a natural inclination to think more strategically (i.e., big picture), whereas others tend to think more tactically (i.e., details). All of this is part of an individual's natural talent.

What is natural talent in strategy?

Natural talent is recurring patterns or tendencies of thought, motivation, or behavior that can be productively applied. It is not based on what school we went to, what subjects we studied, how old we are, or what socioeconomic background we bring with us to the workplace. Recurring patterns are not learned formally or intentionally; instead, they are the product of genetics and experience over time. Talent patterns originate in the subconscious mind; they are simply the ways we naturally think and respond to things, people, and events.

One way to think about natural talent is how some things come easier for some than for others. As a result, when we begin to add in education and societal factors, some will find it easier to excel in a particular job or career, whereas others may struggle. The differences in natural tendencies, both large and nuanced, are infinite. If you want to be a world-class strategist, one requirement is to gain a clear and comprehensive understanding of your natural tendencies (and those of your team) and where they can be used as levers throughout the strategy continuum.

What are skills?

Skills are learned abilities that lead to improved or expanded performance. In contrast to the subconscious origins of talent, skills are intentional and practiced. We may think that Novak Djokovic is a talented tennis player; he does have physical traits that make him formidable on the tennis court. However, without hours, weeks, months, and years of focused practice in the development of specific skills, he would be just another amateur tennis hobbyist, even with all his physical attributes. The key to Djokovic achieving world-class status is that he intentionally developed and practiced skills aligned with his natural talent to pursue goals and a career that captured his passion.

There are three clusters of skills—thinking, achieving, and relating—that are used throughout the stages of the strategy continuum. Although some people may find some of them easier to learn than others, they must all be learned and practiced continually to achieve or maintain world-class status.[10]

Of course, great strategy begins with highly developed thinking skills, which require continuous practice to sharpen our approach.

THINKING SKILLS INCLUDE

- Futuristic thinking: the ability to look beyond present circumstances to see future possibilities
- Conceptual thinking: the ability to think at an abstract level and apply assumption to real life
- Planning and organizing: the ability to create and use logical, systematic processes to achieve goals
- Creativity: the ability to combine ideas in new and unique ways to produce a result
- Continuous learning: the ability to continually gather and integrate new knowledge
- Problem-solving: the ability to analyze, diagnose, and deal with problems effectively
- Decision-making: the ability to make an informed choice from a number of options

Thinking skills are important, but they are not enough to excel in all seven stages of strategy. Achieving skills also play an important role throughout the entire strategy continuum. Achieving skills include

- Self-management: the ability to prioritize goals and decide what needs to be done
- Personal accountability: the ability to take personal responsibility for processes, decisions, actions, and results
- Flexibility: the ability to change plans to match reality
- Resiliency: the ability to persevere and keep going when difficulties arise
- Goal achievement: the ability to execute and achieve desired results

Finally, those who have great relating skills will find greater success engaging other stakeholders throughout the entire process. We have seen relating skills demonstrated again and again with clients who optimize strategy. Those skills include

- Empathy: the ability to identify and understand the perceptions and emotions of others
- Understanding and evaluating others: the ability to recognize the unique strengths and weaknesses of others
- Presenting: the ability to communicate ideas verbally
- Written communication: the ability to articulate a written message in a clear and compelling way
- Diplomacy and tact: the ability to treat others fairly
- Interpersonal: the ability to connect with others in a positive way

- Persuasion: the ability to convince others to change their actions, decisions, opinions, or thinking
- Negotiation: the ability to constructively facilitate agreements between two or more people
- Conflict management: the ability to address and resolve the contradictory interests or values of two or more parties in a high-emotion, low-trust environment
- Teamwork: the ability to work cooperatively with others to achieve group objectives
- Employee development and coaching: the ability to facilitate and support the professional growth of others
- Customer focus: the ability to consistently build long-term relationships based on the delivery of a service, product, or other value

BECOMING A WORLD-CLASS STRATEGIST

Much in the way a world-class athlete creates success over time with consistent, disciplined effort, great strategists must build their insights and competencies layer upon layer. They must practice, experiment, implement, and learn repeatedly to create the knowledge and experience necessary to become world-class.

This process can be broken down into seven relatively simple stages, which we've delineated in figure 1 (on page vi of the preface). As when building any structure, you start with the foundation, the necessary and stable base that you will later build a strategy upon. Without this foundation, the rest of your strategy may crumble. Next, you must have a high level of strategic intelligence—clear and accurate knowledge of the factors inside and outside of your business. At the center of our stage approach is strategic decision-making, which is a crucial skill, and, like any skill, can be learned and improved upon. All these stages build up to execution, putting the strategy into action. But implementation is not the end of any process; you must evaluate the strategy's importance and learn from your successes and mistakes.

However, the strategy process is not always sequential. This is illustrated in the feedback loop of those lessons learned. Although stage 7 is at the end of the process, in reality, strategic evaluation and learning takes place throughout each stage in an iterative and continual fashion. The lessons learned are then fed back to the appropriate stage for the necessary review of the strategy. If, for example, an evaluation is carried out at the end of strategy execution planning (stage 5), and you realize that the environment has changed significantly to create new opportunities, and if the current strategy does not address these opportunities, the strategy team should return to stage 3 to create new strategic options based on the new opportunities and how they interact with the other elements.

Each stage has tools that can be used to produce the output relevant to that stage. To achieve results at each stage, there needs to be a clear understanding of the people and tools involved in your strategy. You'll also notice that outside the core stages, but crucial to each, is effective communication.

Strategy is a process, not an event. When it is done well, the strategic planning phase is surrounded, over time, by great preparation, vigorous debate about what should and should not be part of the strategy commitment, meticulous planning, ongoing focus, regular review, meaningful evaluation, and learning. This model of strategy is your first step in helping your organization thrive in a disruptive world.

TAKING ACTION

WHY

Strategy is a crucial aspect of organizational survival during VUCA events, but it can provide improvement and innovation even during normal operations. It is important to communicate with all contributors that strategy is not an annual event but an ongoing process of continuous learning and execution.

WHAT

Strategy has seven stages, each with tools, people, and results. The work of each stage contributes to a greater clarity, focus, and execution of strategy that results in superior performance. In addition, strategy is strongest when there is alignment among the aspirations of the organization, its departments, and relevant teams and individuals.

WHEN

To optimize strategy, all stakeholders inside an organization (and potential stakeholders outside who will contribute to the organization's success) should be educated and reeducated on the seven stages of strategy throughout the strategy process.

WHO

All employees should have a general understanding of strategy and the seven stages, with deeper training on each of the stages based on their levels of contribution. Whenever possible, stakeholders outside the organization (customers, suppliers, regulators, etc.) should be informed of the strategy if they will make significant contributions or receive significant benefits from its preparation, creation, or optimization.

HOW

Communication methods and media will be identified at the end of each chapter describing a stage in the process. Because of the variety of ways that people receive communication, they should always include written, auditory, and visual communication tactics.

PART 1

PREPARATION

Skills to succeed: futuristic thinking, conceptual thinking, creativity, continuous learning, problem-solving, customer focus

STAGE 1

—■—

THE FOUNDATIONS
OF STRATEGY

An organization's purpose, its long-term vision, and its core values serve as the foundation and the strategy that will lead to its success. These three constituent elements are at the heart of a business and should remain constant and solid, like the foundation of a building. A building cannot be erected until its foundation is strong and stable. Similarly, an organizational strategy cannot be developed and executed until these elements are established and internalized. They feed into and support each other, as seen in figure 1.1.

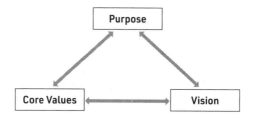

Figure 1.1. The foundations of strategy.

To determine what your organization's foundation should be, you first need to know the essence of the organization's identity, or brand. Next, you must decide where you want the organization to go, what future state it's moving toward. These questions represent wide and varied conversations within the company and with external stakeholders; they should include storytelling about the company's past, what the organization is about, and what it aspires to become and achieve in the future.

For example, you want your organization to transition from state A (its current position—say, a restaurant chain with two locations) at time T_1 (now) to state B (a multistate franchise operation) at time T_2 (the long term; e.g., 10 years). This transition takes place because state A is the current reality, and the organization has identified opportunities to transition to a superior state (state B). The transition is achieved through strategy—the continuous adjustment of goals and actions that is represented by the line between the two states. The strategy will enable the organization to improve its performance from P_1 (making a small profit at those two locations) at T_1 (state A) to P_2 (enough revenue to expand) at a future time, T_2 (state B). The vision is only realizable at T_2 and is not available before then (change takes time). The core values are everywhere within the box, and we cannot achieve the vision without these core values and purpose.

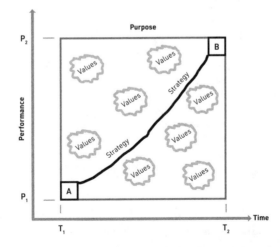

Figure 1.2. Performance over time, built on the foundational elements of strategy.

Figure 1.2 shows strategy in action: a line connecting the current state of the company with its goal. However, arriving at the goal takes time, and it must be surrounded and supported by a foundation of purpose, values, and vision.

In our consulting, we often work with organizations that assume their purpose, vision, and values based on past documents rather than taking the time to discuss, reflect, and refine them. Their attitude toward purpose and values is often, "Well, that's the way we have always done it, and there doesn't seem to be a reason to change." Their attitude about vision is often, "We are just going to keep doing what we've been doing and hope for the best. Besides, who can predict the future these days?"

One of the companies Ron worked with developed a purpose statement that read, "Improving the quality of life through principles of individual wellness and promoting the highest principles of free enterprise." Its core values were: respect for every individual, a commitment to excellence, a dedication to customer service, and promoting success through personal initiative. This purpose statement and these core values initially evolved from several conversations during a weekend retreat in April 1989 in Sun Valley, Idaho. Core ideas also emerged from these discussions. It took several months to refine them and to gain support from the majority of the employees. Next, Ron worked with them to develop a 10-year vision that included product development and market growth. The goal was to grow the business in current markets and expand into new countries. When this goal was adopted, the company's leaders didn't know how they would achieve it. However, the goal provided clarity as they made decisions and encountered both challenges and opportunities along the way. During this time, the company introduced several new products and expanded into eight new countries, which resulted in a tripling of the company's revenue and a customer base growth of more than 100,000.

PURPOSE

A crucial piece of an organization's foundation is its purpose; it is *why* the company exists. Organizational purpose is often described in a mission or purpose statement, which answers core questions about the company. For any organization, this is a good place to start. For example, to create a purpose statement, you and your leadership team must clearly define why the company exists, what the business will do to accomplish this purpose, who its customers are, and what those customers value. We tend to use the terms "purpose" and "mission" differently: the purpose is why the organization exists and the mission is the organization's purpose applied to current customer needs—what it will *do* to fulfill the purpose. This is an important distinction that has opened up new insights for us and our clients.

Why does your company exist?

Purpose gives an organization its heart. Verne Harnish[1] argues that an organization's purpose can be discerned from the following two questions.

What difference are we making in the world?

A primary way to determine what difference your company is making in the world is to explore who is affected by its existence. One of Ron's clients, a family-owned agribusiness, started by asking several generations of their family, then their employees (both full time and seasonal), then their buyers, brokers, distributors, grocers, and, finally, consumers, what difference they thought they were making in the world. Through this discussion, the organization became more aware of the wide scope of its impact—its decisions, investments, values, and results all had the potential for significant impact. It was decided that the difference the company makes in the world is connecting farmers with the tools, machinery, and support they need to thrive in today's agriculture market.

Why would our customers, or the world, miss us if we weren't around?

Would anyone miss your company if it were gone, and—more importantly—why? These questions are both easy and hard to answer. Initially, most organizations begin by meeting one or more specific needs in the communities they seek to serve. There are a variety of motivations that lead an entrepreneur to launch a new business: "I want to be my own boss"; "I want to create wealth"; "I have a new product or service and I want to control how it is produced or delivered"; or "I couldn't find a job that provided for my family, so I decided to create the job for myself." These initial motivations drive the creation of the product or services you provide to your customers and the world, and they are what would be missing if you were gone.

Occasionally, an entrepreneur has a large vision that can only be pursued through a new business. For example, one of our clients who started his first business boldly proclaimed, "I want to cure cancer!" In the beginning, answers come easily because of the close connection between the founders of a company and its customers (or constituents, in the case of nongovernment or government entities). As organizations mature and seek to discover—and then pursue— their greatest potential, these questions deserve greater attention. It is highly unlikely that Bill Gates, Steve Jobs, Jeff Bezos, or Elon Musk started their businesses with the same purpose statement they have today. Instead, as they and their businesses grew, reasons for existing as an organization grew as well and needed to be clarified and expanded. The original purpose of Amazon, Google, or Alibaba was embryonic at the beginning, and each has grown in scope and clarity along the way. So how do you identify the seed of purpose and bring greater clarity for the future?

An organization's purpose is often derived from the purpose of its founder or leadership. In private firms, this is often evident in the founder's story of why they began the business or determined by the CEO or board of directors. It is some fundamental story of why the company was built and what greater effect it would achieve in the world.

Dr. Evans runs a company called The Innovator's Advantage, LLC. After growing up in Kenya and coming to the United States for university and postgraduate studies, he rediscovered a passion for innovation, which he remembers being present from his earliest years working on the family farm. As he pursued this passion academically and then as an employee of a global technology company, it became evident that he would only be happy owning a company that was a catalyst for innovation for his clients and their organizations. This would be the core purpose for his company's existence. This seed of purpose has driven him to continually ask, "What difference are we making in the world?" and "Why would our customers or the world miss us if we weren't around?" Today, Dr. Evans can answer these questions with clarity, conviction, and passion.

If your founder's story was never recorded or has been lost over time with the company's growth, write a new one. You may need to interview your organization's founder, or you may need someone to interview you if you are the founder. What drove them or you to create the company? What greater purpose do you hope to achieve by offering your product or service? In a formal, public organization, the purpose can often be captured in the instruments that established it, such as a law or by-laws.

After thinking deeply about the way your organization can change the world, the void its absence would create, and its superhero origin story, you should have a good idea of why your company exists. Describe it in a sentence—and write it down!

What does your business do?

We also encourage you to progress from simple to complex explanations when defining what your business does. Think about how you would describe your business to an eight-year-old. For example, "We put new rubber on tires so that trucks are safe and can go farther without having to worry about their tires." (This was the purpose of a company Ron co-owned with his father.) It may not sound exciting, but it's the best place to begin.

There is actually a lot hidden in this simple statement, such as technology, material science, engineering, manufacturing, locations, customer service, and economics. At its core, a business—or any organization—exists to create value for others. When explained simply, you have answered *what*. Later in strategy, you will spend more time defining *how*. Marketing campaigns seek to create and communicate an answer that is much more aspirational and compelling. However, when discussing purpose, it is better to start simple and work on the magic of wordsmithing later. The current purpose statement for Ron's organization, Price Associates, is: "We work with leaders to help them think more clearly, get more of the right things done, and have healthier, more productive relationships."

Who are your customers?

The purpose of nearly any business is to create and satisfy customers, and the business is necessarily defined by customers' wants, needs, and values[2]:

Management has to ask which of the consumer's wants are not adequately satisfied by the products or services offered him today. The ability to ask this question and to answer it correctly usually makes the difference between a growth company and one that depends for its development on the rising tide of the economy or the industry. But whoever contents himself to rise with the tide will also fall with it.

A fundamental part of meeting your customers' needs is understanding who they are. What are their pain points? What do they lack or want that your company can provide?

If you are an established entity, you should start by defining your current customers and why they work with you. List all the attributes they have that you can think of: Where are they located? What do they do? If they have customers, why do their customers buy from them? What size are they (employees, revenue, other measures)? What other demographics can you identify about your current customers?

Next, ask who your customers should be in the future. Go back through all the data you collected about your current customers and ask yourself what, why, when, and how they will buy from you in the future.

What do your customers value?

What problems do you solve for your current customers? Why do they choose you over your competitors? What reasons will they have to remain your customers in the future? Are you satisfied with your current customers, both individually and overall, as a portfolio of customers? Why? Why not? After capturing as many insights about your current customers as you can, look for things they have in common. Organize them according to the amount of success you have, or expect to have in the future, doing business with them. Rank your customers according to their revenue potential, their future revenue potential, the degree to which you are able to do your best work with and for them, and how well they align with your fundamental purpose.

Organizational purpose must be shared with the business's stakeholders, especially its customers, because, as Simon Sinek affirms,[3] customers don't buy the products and services you provide; they buy *why* you do it. If your purpose is unclear or fickle, you will likely have difficulty building or keeping a loyal customer base.

Today, customers can buy many different brands of smartphones, tablets, and computers. In spite of tremendous competition, the best customers tend to develop a lasting loyalty for one company or provider. For Apple, that loyalty is often about design and the feeling of being part of something special. Its customers identify with the late Steve Jobs's value of elevating individual empowerment in his "rage against the machine." In the most current 10 commercials for Apple products, the message is always much more about the *why* than the *what* or *how*. They're all important, but the *why* creates loyalty and what marketers refer to as the "*lifetime value of the customer.*"

The connection of your company's purpose with a clear set of values goes beyond just the customer. If your organizational purpose becomes hazy, it also becomes difficult to harness the creativity, loyalty, and capabilities of your employees and even your investors, board members, and external partners. This crucial element underlines the critical importance of getting the purpose right and sharing it among all the stakeholders of the organization. If your employees and other stakeholders embody the purpose in their day-to-day activities (as you and company decisions should), productivity is likely to substantially increase. Indeed, as Verne Harnish says in his book *Scaling Up*,[4] "If you ignite and capture their [your employees[1]] hearts, not just their heads,

---

1   Our emphasis.

they will give you 40% more discretionary effort." You don't expect loyalty; you earn it through a clear and consistent purpose.

Creating a purpose statement

A good purpose statement has five basic requirements: (1) It must state the reason for the company's existence and define its identity. (2) It (typically) must be created by the founder or leadership team of the organization—typically the CEO or the board. (3) It must endure; that is, it must remain valid for a long period of time, often for the entire life of an organization. (4) It must be shared by the customers and by all employees, shareholders, and outside partners. (5) It must guide the company's day-to-day actions and interactions with those stakeholders. The development and execution of a solid corporate strategy is one of the mechanisms that bring the organization's purpose to life.

We recommend the following procedure, modified from Harnish's proposal, to create your own purpose statement. Begin by creating a team and have them go through the following activities.

First, have your team answer the question, *Why was the company originally created*? Going back to Ron's work with the senior leadership team at the agricultural business previously discussed, they had never created a formal strategy, even though they had been in business for more than 50 years. Ron interviewed the current leader of the business in front of the leadership team and asked him what had motivated his father to start the company. Although the main reason was agricultural-based, the leader's response indicated that the underlying purpose of the business was the pursuit of the American Dream. Upon further inquiry, Ron learned that the founder's idea of the American Dream meant owning a business that provided for his family; providing employment opportunities for others (who he almost viewed as members of his family); applying their combined efforts to grow high-quality, high-nutrition crops; and constantly pursuing excellence in the stewardship of his land and equipment.

These were deeply meaningful reasons for the founder, and they provided resilience when going through the ups and downs of a challenging business landscape that was dominated by market fluctuations outside of his control. Ron later discovered that much of the success of this family business came from the sterling reputation it had with buyers, distributors, and grocers. In the case of this business, the consumer was a more distant customer—still important when it came to the quality of its products but secondary to those who gave access to the consumer by stocking their store's shelves.

Ron's client regularly told the story of the family's joy in building the American Dream into their branding, displays, social media, and video storytelling. Over time, everyone in the supply chain developed a loyalty to this company, which made this family-owned agribusiness the provider of choice.

A powerful purpose tends to revolve around a single word or idea that is more easily remembered and acted upon. Although it may sound vague to us, the client's purpose of "living the American Dream" was deep with meaning for everyone associated with the business. Once you have a preliminary draft of your organization's purpose statement, you would next reconfigure it to focus on a central word or idea, such as a service or innovation. For the agribusiness, that was "the American Dream" related to "farming."

Next, you'll expand that single-word purpose into a phrase or two. For Ron's client, their purpose statement became "We exist to build and perpetuate a family farm agribusiness." This was not a marketing slogan (they also have one of those that is customercentric). This was a brief, poignant statement of why they exist.

You would next present the draft purpose for discussion and adoption by key organizational actors. Such a process can be facilitated by a strategy expert, who will often coax more feedback and ideation from key players than an individual with organizational responsibilities might. Ron's client had small group discussions with employees throughout the company, as well as with its bankers, family members, and advisory board. When appropriate, more informal discussions also took place in social settings with customers, such as during a golf outing or a shared meal.

Here is the agribusiness purpose statement in its totality:

> We exist to build and perpetuate a family farm agribusiness. We are committed to cultivating excellence and will be #1 or #2 in each of our business units. We will provide our customers with the highest quality products and services. We will treat our customers, employees, and community with respect and integrity.

Note that this purpose statement should not be used as a template. The statement should be unique to each organization. The power comes from creating a purpose statement that results from deep discussions, including the founder's story and their current sense of responsibility and pride in the business.

Evergreen purpose

The wants, needs, and values of customers change depending on the environment, and this is why we distinguish between purpose and mission. While maintaining a strong sense of purpose, a business should be able to pivot to serve these changing desires without adjusting its reason for existence. What an organization does to serve its customers—for example, delivering certain products and services—is merely an expression of its wider mission. The organization's purpose, on the other hand, should be evergreen, consistent, and unchanging. In addition to defining the organization's identity, the purpose statement guides its development over time. The challenge for leaders is to recognize how to translate purpose into practice, which is done through planning, strategy, and execution.

A purpose statement defines your organization's identity, its reason for being. When you have a well-articulated sense of purpose, you have the first piece necessary to build a firm foundation that provides clear guidance for all significant decisions and actions. It also establishes a point of reference for developing strategy, planning its execution, and actually implementing it.

CORE VALUES

An organization's core values describe the principles and standards that guide its behaviors and decisions. This is often translated as corporate culture, or "the way we do things around here," but we are referring more specifically to that small set of beliefs that are most important to the company, the backbone in guiding day-to-day interactions, actions, and decisions. Core values constitute the character or personality that an organization aspires to reflect in all its decisions and actions. If purpose is Harnish's[5] heart of an organization, core values are its soul. This organizational personality is crucial in helping us pursue our purpose and realize our vision.

An organization's core values describe its commitments to how it treats people (employees, customers, vendors, shareholders, and society) and its commitments to its purpose (ethical conduct, standards of performance, and contributing to a better world).

Organizations typically list their values in generic words, such as *integrity, customer service, teamwork,* and so on, and hang those words on office walls, in the lobby, or in other prominent places. In such situations, the values are often developed as a matter of routine practice—to tick a box, so to speak. This, however, misses the importance and power of core values as the central aspirations of the organization.

To avoid the generic list of nice-to-have words or phrases that don't mean much to anyone, you need to answer the following questions: Do your core values distinguish you from your competitors? Does everyone in the organization seek to live the core values; that is, do they use them to bind their behaviors and guide their decisions? Can you—or *will* you—fire your most valued employee or leader for a violation of these values? Can your employees put their own careers in jeopardy by not upholding these values?

Before dedicating his career to help leaders of other organizations, Ron was the president of a company with operations in eight different countries. He regularly spoke with his employees about the importance of their core values. His two primary responsibilities as the senior leader of the organization were to keep the organization true to its purpose and to build a culture based on its core values.

During his tenure, there were some employees who decided to test his resolve. He explained that most mistakes or failures could be forgiven and considered opportunities for growth. But intentional violation of core values was dealt with firmly and swiftly. The fastest way to have Ron help someone find employment elsewhere, especially if they were in a leadership role, was by flaunting a disregard for the core values.

Creating a set of core values

A good set of core values for organizations includes starting with a small set of beliefs (typically three to five) that represent what is expected of its behaviors and that guide its actions and decisions. These core values will define your corporate personality and distinguish you from similar organizations. Everyone—from the CEO to the new intern—must seek to live these core values every day. As the soul of the organization, core values are a key determinant of successful execution of strategy.

How, then, do we create and internalize core values that are the true soul of the organization? After all, what gets rewarded will get repeated. Core values that are intrinsic expressions of the best versions of ourselves will challenge and govern our behaviors. We propose the following simple steps.

Examine what values seem to have guided your organization in the past. These values could have been handed down by the founder or may have evolved naturally from the purpose of the organization. If you are establishing core values for the first time, a good starting point is considering the values of the founder.

In the case of the agribusiness Ron worked with, the discussions led to adopting the following core values:

- Integrity
- Pride in excellence
- Passion
- Teamwork
- Accountability

Each of these values had a precise definition, which we are not sharing because of the strategic advantage these core values continue to provide Ron's client. There are no "perfect" core values. What is important is the value they represent to you in how you operate your business and the competitive advantage they will give you in the marketplace.

There are numerous options for starting points and ways to brainstorm core values. For example, in working with another client, Ron asked the leadership team to browse through a stack of magazines from a variety of interests and pull out pictures that represented the values of their organization. This led to a discussion about what those pictures represented, which eventually led to narrowing down a list of three to five potential values that everyone on the team agreed constituted the soul of the organization.

This client adopted the following core values as a result of the exercise:

- A God-centered, God-driven business (and they were a for-profit business)
- Quality work
- People
- Partnerships
- Environment

Once again, each of these core values had precise definitions that will remain confidential. What is interesting is that the client's leadership team simply looked through a stack of magazines, which then generated rigorous discussions and, finally, strongly held core values.

Prof. Tim facilitated a strategy project for a school and asked the client to disregard the existing values and start afresh. After identifying four core values, Prof. Tim challenged the participants to define the core values in their own words and discuss how these values were expressed in their jobs. Each definition had to be validated with real experiences that brought them to life. Through this process, conversations changed, and people began to recognize how certain behaviors where not aligned with the newly defined values. This was the starting point of owning the core values and using them to guide the behaviors of everyone.

You can also direct the discussion from the bottom up (employees to leadership) rather than from the top down (leadership to employees). Ron participated in the early stages of a pharmaceutical IPO that was the result of breaking away from a large, global organization. The strategy team started with a list of potential values and asked its employees to identify which values resonated most for them and why. The organization eventually adopted five core values with a high degree of employee support.

This company, currently traded on the New York Stock Exchange, adopted the following core values:

- Our colleagues make the difference.
- Always do the right thing.
- Be customer obsessed.
- Run it like you own it.
- We are one company (with many business units and in many countries).

Ron was once told by this company's head of strategy that analysts don't care about core values. They only care about share value, increasing revenue, and decreasing costs. At first, this was discouraging to hear. However, this company has continued to grow and excel, in large part because of how its core values shape everything else it does. The company's employees don't always live up to the high standards expressed through these values, but they remain accountable to and inspired by them.

Articulate each core value in one or two sentences and anchor each with an actual story of an instance in which an employee or team lived that value. For one of our businesses, we have adopted three core values with the following definitions:

- **Seeing clearly.** We will intentionally grow our self-awareness and help others do the same. This core value will result in continuous innovation and successful strategies for growth as individuals, as teams, and as a thriving business.

- **Synergy through collaboration.** The total effect is greater than the sum of the parts. We will seek collaboration and interdependence with humility and a commitment to serve each other with respect, empathy, inclusion, fairness, and a love for diversity. This will result in promoting a strong, respectful, and empowering culture for ourselves and for those we serve.

- **Making a difference.** We are passionate and purposeful about making a difference for ourselves and also in the lives of others and the organizations they serve. This will result in elevated levels of performance, fulfillment, and joy.

Next, you will integrate these core values into the performance management system. This means there will be rewards for people who live the core values and sanctions for those who violate them. For example, Ron held a contest recognizing essays that included stories and anecdotes relating to the organization's core values in one of the companies he led. There were also additional expressions of recognition when employees were observed using the core values in tough decision-making circumstances. One example was printing company "money" and allowing anyone in the organization to give it to other employees when they observed them making decisions and responding in alignment with the core values. The company money could then be used to purchase a wide variety of items, including company-branded clothing, products, gift certificates to local restaurants, and so on. This ongoing recognition brought consistent focus to being governed by company values in a variety of circumstances.

Leaders and managers should regularly communicate their core values in multiple ways. For example, Prof. Tim facilitated the development of strategy for a high school as part of his corporate social responsibility. When the core values were agreed upon, he challenged the music teacher, who was one of the enthusiastic participants in determining those values, to create a school anthem based on them. She gathered a few music students and began writing the song. Once the song was approved by the school's administration, it was sung every Friday during the school parade (something that is quite common in Kenyan schools). This communicated and reinforced these values to the students, faculty, and staff on a weekly basis and helped them internalize the school's strong culture.

VISION

Vision represents how an organization wants to be perceived in the future. It is an expression of the desired end state, a dream of the company's ultimate goals. As Walt Disney said, "If you can dream it, you can do it." Vision represents what success will look like in 10 or 20 years. This is our end point (T_2) in figure 1.2. The role of vision in the organization is to provide long-term focus, to challenge all employees to reach for a state that represents superior performance, and to inspire a compelling future.

There are two main schools of thought on what constitutes an organization's vision. One is the inspirational school, where the vision is meant to inspire. Here, the end state is never achieved, but it acts as an enduring inspiration for all stakeholders, a constant prize just out of reach. You can think of it as a mirage—the closer you get to it, the farther away it moves.

The second school of thought is aspirational. In this case, the vision should have a concrete goal that can—and should—be achieved. Jim Collins's model[6] is the classic example. He argues that a well-crafted vision statement should include a big, hairy, audacious goal (BHAG) that challenges even well-performing organizations to become better. The classic example of BHAG is Jack Welch's challenge for every GE business unit to become number one or two in its industry.

In our opinion, both are needed: A vision statement needs to be both inspirational and aspirational. One of our clients has started multiple biotech companies over the past two decades. All have been successful in creating and satisfying customers through novel products and services (aspirational), but they have also each held on to an over-arching vision to "cure cancer, once and for all" (inspirational).

One of our own businesses has an ambitious, aspirational BHAG. A 10-year goal (a true global presence, over tenfold growth, and so on) that is guided by an inspirational vision to change the world through growing great leaders.

Creating a vision statement

The process of developing a long-term vision can be messy, if it is to be done properly. In some situations, senior leadership may be clear about their long-term vision. In such circumstances, the next step is to share this vision with other stakeholders for review and ownership. However, from our consultancy experience, many leaders are challenged by envisioning, on their own, their organization's ultimate goal of success. We therefore recommend facilitation by an experienced strategy expert.

Ron has used a workshop environment with several different clients. He asks the participants go through the following steps.

Think back

Think back 20 years and identify everything that has changed over this period of time, in your organization or in the world around you. Often, this exercise identifies changes in leadership, employees, products, services, customers, business models, or technologies that didn't exist or hadn't been implemented 20 years ago. Looking back is much easier than looking forward. We have found this is an effective way to help people begin thinking long term before taking on the more challenging work of looking forward.

Identify trends

Identify and discuss key trends that are likely to change your business or the world over the next 20 years. Examples can include demographics, technology, globalism, health care, politics or geopolitics, and so on.

Ron used this approach with a food service business. He started this phase of developing vision by sharing anticipated breakthroughs in 3D printing, flying cars, artificial intelligence, and machine learning. The client immediately started seeing how all these breakthroughs would force them to rethink some of the core activities of their business. What if 3D printing could eventually create meals on site? What if there were opportunities in the future for designer foods based on nutritional analysis and the preferences of individual customers? What impact would autonomous flying vehicles have on their business operations? These are just a few examples of how, as Peter Diamandis and Steven Kotler write in their book *The Future Is Faster Than You Think*, "we will experience 100 years of change in the next 10 years."[7]

Brainstorm

Identify and discuss 20 new things that could mark your reality in 20 years.[8] It is important to visualize this reality in your mind and then put it into a drawing. These new things might include technology, such as the Internet of Things, artificial intelligence, machine learning, 3D printing, material science, robotics, displacement and retraining of workers, augmented reality, virtual reality, and any other number of innovations. The future of demographics might include shifting buying power of various generations (traditionalists, boomers, Gen Xers, millennials, iGen, etc.), shifts in global influence from developing nations and in ethnic groups' population size, and trends in the definition of family. New ideas in transportation might include autonomous vehicles, high-speed land mass transit, and new forms of flying transportation. You might even consider governance models: new solutions that replace or advance capitalism, socialism, democracy, communism, etc., or new approaches to taxation, financing of infrastructure, health care, and retirement.

There will be trends that are more specific and more impactful on your organization that can be identified by reading industry or sector-specific literature, attending association events, and following industry thought leaders on social media.

Group work

Next, break up into two groups. Group 1 should identify 10 things that you want the outside world (your customers, competitors, suppliers, community, shareholders, etc.) to say about you in 20 years. How would they describe your company? This includes the products or services you will produce, where you will exist, what impact you will have, and what they will say about you to their colleagues. Group 2 should identify 10 things you want your employees (and their families) to be saying about you in 20 years. This includes the employee experience, the role of technology, and career opportunities.

Have these two groups present and discuss their lists. Specific attention should be given to identifying which aspirations will align with hard trends and which will align with soft trends.[9] Note: It has been our experience that most organizations overestimate what they can accomplish in one year and underestimate what they can accomplish in 20 years.

Write it down

Select a small team, with members drawn from the two groups, to integrate the outputs for a vision statement. In 2006, one of our clients developed several areas of focus for their 10-year vision (see the following list). This is the same year the iPhone was introduced, so it is interesting to compare their vision in 2006 to the results they achieved by 2016. We have adapted these descriptions to protect the confidentiality of our client.

OUR EXTERNAL 10-YEAR VISION

- We will maintain and improve our status as the premier provider in our region.
- We will expand our experience in larger, more complex projects.
- We will acquire related businesses or form strategic partnerships to ensure a consistent supply of materials and expertise in our business.
- We will expand into new markets, both sectors and geographical.
- We will develop specific additional in-house services and expertise to increase the value we deliver to our customers.

- We will double our market share in our defined markets.
- We will expand our investments into a variety of fixed assets that will provide steady, recurring cash flow and profit.
- We will increase the value and scope of our brand.

OUR INTERNAL 10-YEAR VISION

- We will strengthen our culture through offering flex time, four-day workweeks, and work-from-home options by nurturing a growth mindset throughout the company and by deeply integrating our company values throughout the employee population.
- We will strengthen our financial position through creating high-paying jobs, continuing to increase our profitability, and achieving preferred customer status from our vendors by providing accurate and prompt payments.
- We will strengthen our infrastructure through leadership development, continuity across all our office locations, standardized policies and procedures, and integration of total quality management across the company.
- We will strengthen our technologies through improved communication systems, software integration across all departments, increased in-house expertise and leadership in technology, and optimizing our use of video conferencing.
- We will strengthen our human resources through continuous and relevant training, maintaining competitive employee benefits, compensating employees on the high end in our markets, continuously improving our hiring

practices, and consistently applying our employee-related policies and procedures.

Once again, the point is not to have a perfect vision but to have a vision that will guide the development of strategy as you move into stage 2 in the journey of strategy. Our client experienced significant disruptions during the great recession of 2008–2010. They could have easily collapsed, but their resilience and their 10-year vision helped guide their decision-making. Today, they are larger and more successful than ever before.

Establish buy-in

Send the vision statements to all participants. Have them think through all the choices before the next session. After a week or two, convene the next session to consider the final vision from the list of candidates. Which of the statements represents more aspirational BHAGS, and which ones will be more inspirational?

Vision into narrative

Finally, just as with purpose and core values, you must communicate your vision to your company's stakeholders. Create a compelling story of the vision to be used, which will communicate this state of success in the future. Our client's document was clear, compelling, and brief. On one page, they listed the external 10-year vision and provided more detail than we have listed under each area of focus. On the second page, they listed the internal 10-year vision with additional detail for each area of focus. Before going through this process, the senior leaders lacked the confidence to create a long-term vision for the company. Like many others, they had some sense of what to expect over the next two or three years (they were actually quite good at this) but not much further. As a result of creating this 10-year vision, we observed a dramatic increase in enthusiasm, commitment, and clarity for how they could bring their vision into reality.

We do a considerable amount of work in the technology sector, where the environment changes so fast that most organizational leaders don't believe a 10-year vision is possible or useful. However, we have repeatedly demonstrated that this practice of creating a longer-term vision influences how leaders develop strategy in the short term. It isn't as important whether the 10-year vision is realized as imagined as it is important for creating a larger context of the future to improve the strategy decisions being made today.

The resulting vision needs to be effective in helping bring clarity to where you are going, a critical first step in developing strategy. An effective vision must include all the following features:

- **Imaginable**: It must convey a picture of what the future will look like.
- **Desirable**: It should appeal to the long-term interests of employees, customers, and other stakeholders.
- **Feasible**: It must include a realistic and attainable long-term goal.
- **Focused**: It must be clear enough to provide guidance in decision-making.
- **Flexible**: It must be general enough to allow individual initiative and alternative responses to changes in both the internal and external environments.
- **Communicable**: It must be easy to communicate and successfully explained within five minutes.

A vision defines a successful state in the future—your dream of your company's success. It also inspires, motivates, and challenges. More importantly, it provides a basis for developing the other aspects of your strategy—themes, objectives, goals, and action plans.

TAKING ACTION

WHY

The foundation of purpose, values, and vision provides stability and a framework for the development of strategy in an organization. When done well, these foundational factors will create a unity of purpose, a commitment to the best-version-of-ourselves conduct, and a compelling direction for the development of strategy. When these factors are missing or ambiguous, unity, commitment, and clear direction will often be lacking.

WHAT

Purpose should describe why we exist as an organization, values should define the character of the organization, and vision should describe a preferable future state that reflects superior performance and value for all relevant stakeholders.

WHEN

The purpose, values, and vision of the organization should be communicated repeatedly throughout the life of the organization. Specifically, these foundational factors should be connected to all discussions throughout the seven stages of strategy.

WHO

Everyone in the organization should be able to articulate purpose, values, and vision. In addition, external stakeholders should be familiar with them and resonate with their enduring nature.

HOW

Because purpose, values, and vision are key intrinsic components of an organization's identity, there should be multiple ways of continually communicating them. Whenever possible, this should include creative, artistic, visual, auditory, and written forms of communication. In every case, methods and styles of communication should inspire pride, a strong sense of ownership, and intrinsic (emotional) commitment to the organization.

KEY TAKEAWAYS

It is not always the case that the three foundational elements are developed from scratch. Given their enduring nature, it is often the case that they are reviewed and confirmed when they will continue to serve the organization well.

Throughout our journey in this book, we'll learn the key requirements of an effective strategy in three main categories: the tools you need to succeed, the people who will help you get there, and the results of your work.

TOOLS

- The characteristics of a good purpose statement
- How to develop a purpose statement
- The characteristics of a good set of core values
- Guidelines to create and internalize core values
- Characteristics of an effective vision
- How to create that effective vision

PEOPLE

- Founders, others with a history in the organization
- Key leaders and influencers
- Those who see the organization as serving a purpose that transcends self-interest

RESULTS

- Purpose
- Core values
- A long-term vision

STAGE 2

—■—

BUILDING STRATEGIC INTELLIGENCE

Since its introduction by Mayer and Salovey[1] and its subsequent popularization by Goleman,[2] the concept of emotional intelligence has been used to study organizational behavior and organizational psychology.[3] At its core, emotional intelligence is a person's ability to recognize their own emotions and those of others. In a social situation, you can use emotional intelligence to guide your interactions with other people. You adjust a discussion, an argument, or a presentation to appeal to positive emotions and allay negative ones.

Applying emotional intelligence to an organization is similar, although we'll call it *strategic intelligence* to differentiate the two. You determine the effect your decisions will have on the internal environment (your corporate culture) and on the external environment (interactions with your customers and competitors), and create a strategy to drive positive change and avoid negative outcomes.

Two related and crucial aspects of strategic intelligence are your stakeholders and your abilities (strengths, limitations, opportunities, and challenges), and we'll discuss analyzing both as well.

INTERNAL ENVIRONMENT ASSESSMENT

An internal environment assessment helps us understand the key internal drivers for change. The result of this analysis will be a comprehensive understanding of the organization's competence or strengths and limitations.[2]

The internal dimensions of emotional intelligence are *self-awareness*, the ability to recognize and understand your mood, emotions, drives, and values; *self-regulation*, the ability to control or redirect disruptive impulses and moods and the propensity to suspend judgment and think before acting; and *motivation*, the passion to work for reasons that go beyond the external drive for knowledge, utility, surroundings, others, power, or methodology, which are based on internal drive or propensity to pursue goals with energy and persistence. These three dimensions can be used to analyze the internal environment of an organization as well, although we refer to them as *organizational awareness*, *organizational discipline*, and *organizational energy*, respectively.

In these three dimensions, the purpose of analysis is to determine the organization's core strengths and key limitations. The three dimensions of the internal environment of an organization, together with their lower-level components, are illustrated in figure 2.1

The three dimensions are in constant, dynamic interaction with each other. Therefore, a change in one dimension may trigger a change in the other two. For example, a change in organizational culture might necessitate changes in the tools that regulate organizational discipline, such as organizational processes and practices.

---

2   We use the term "limitations" instead of the traditional term "weaknesses" because the latter tends to have a negative connotation and because we cannot know whether it will constitute a true weakness until we have determined our strategic themes.

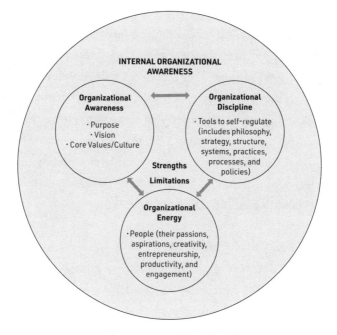

Figure 2.1. Internal organizational awareness dimensions.

Organizational awareness

Organizational awareness concerns the organization's purpose and vision. It is also about the shared attitudes and beliefs within the company, what we refer to as organizational culture. This aspect largely results from the internalization of shared core values among the leadership and staff. The term "awareness" is just what it sounds like: we want an accurate picture of the company's purpose, vision, and culture—not the idealized image the CEO may wish the company to reflect. The goal of our analysis is clarity, accuracy, and realism, as opposed to either unrealistic optimism or pessimism.

Review relevant documents

We'll begin our analysis by reviewing your existing strategic plan and code of ethics, provided you have them. How clear and current are these documents? How are they currently used? Are they referred to often, or have they been forgotten? Are they considered relevant or outdated? Were they created by the current leadership team, or were they inherited from a previous administration? What can we carry forward from these documents? What needs updating or replacing? If these documents don't exist, foundational work will need to be completed to guide your creation and optimization of strategy.

Interview key stakeholders

You'll want to interview all (or a representative sample) of your internal stakeholders. This includes leaders at all levels, key employees, past and present board members, and especially those leaders you think may be tasked with driving change in the organization. You'll want to ask general questions but also questions about the stakeholders' understanding of the purpose of the organization, its strategic direction, how well the organization assesses its own performance, and what the key strengths and limitations of the organization are.

Here are a few examples:

GENERAL QUESTIONS

- What are we doing right in our business?
- What are we doing wrong in our business?
- What should we start doing in our business?
- What should we stop doing in our business?

- How deep and broad does our understanding reach in having a clear, unbiased picture of our current internal situation?

- Does everyone understand their roles, levels of authority, and responsibilities?

PURPOSE

- Are we clear about our purpose at the senior leadership level and throughout the employee population?

- Is our purpose defined specifically? Is it concise and easy to understand?

- Does our purpose resonate with and capture the passion of our employees?

- Is our purpose understood and shared by our customers, vendors, and industry partners?

- Is our purpose dynamic and relevant?

- Does our purpose point us toward gaining or maintaining a competitive advantage?

STRATEGIC DIRECTION

- How much ownership do employees take regarding the organization's purpose and long-term vision?

- Does the organization cascade its purpose, vision, values, and goals throughout the organization to make them relevant and meaningful to every single person's contributions?

MONITORING AND EVALUATION

- Are we reviewing the purpose, vision, values, and goals often enough to maintain relevance in the dance between individual and organizational purpose, values, and aspirations?

STRENGTHS AND LIMITATIONS

- What are the strengths in our purpose, long-term vision, and values?

- Is our strategic direction better than those of our competitors or potential competitors?

- How could we leverage our core strengths in our purpose, vision, and values?

- What competencies do we lack that limit our impact in fulfilling our purpose and vision?

- What are our key limitations in our strategic direction?

- Are there limitations that we should turn into strengths?

The purpose of these questions is to ascertain how aware the organization is of its current internal realities and how deep this awareness is embedded throughout the organization. Whenever possible, we recommend having an external strategy expert conduct these interviews because of the anonymity that allows for more candid answers and because of their expertise in probing for greater insights through great questions and unbiased listening.

Organizational discipline

The extent to which the organization has tools to help it self-regulate or self-manage is referred to as organizational discipline. These abilities allow the organization to increase capacities to deliver value over time. These tools include philosophy, strategy, structure, systems, policies, practices, processes, procedures, models, quality management, talent management, risk management, and intellectual property, among others. Organizational discipline also includes the awareness and intelligence to recognize disruptive events and manage or redirect them to minimize distraction or leakage and, when appropriate, use them to create new organizational competencies.

We list the methodology and tools that we propose be used to appraise organizational discipline in the following sections.

Review relevant documents

Review the relevant existing documents for the pertinent and key tools for self-regulation or management previously listed. The following questions will help you evaluate the documents:

- What documents do we have that describe philosophy, strategy, structure, systems, policies, practices, processes, procedures, models, quality management, talent management, risk management, and our management of intellectual property?

- How consistently do we use these disciplines and practices to optimize our work, continuously improve our quality and productivity, and stay prepared for disruptive or opportunistic events?

- What level of resilience or capacity do these disciplines have before gaps appear? How much can we expand or contract before our systems begin to break down?

- How are we managing the different kinds and levels of risk in our organization?

- How prepared are we as an organization to respond to a wide variety of potential crises?

- What crisis management plans do we have in place, and how do we practice the skills and activities required to successfully activate them?

- What type of crisis communication plans do we have, and how well prepared are our people to implement them?

- How strong is our financial management, including enabling technologies, accurate and timely record keeping, financial analysis and performance improvement, revenue and profit forecasting, and treasury management (including banking relationships, currency management, asset management, liabilities management, investment strategies, regulatory compliance, and shareholder relations)?

Interview key stakeholders

As with the previous analysis, we'll need to interview key internal stake-holders. Here is a sampling of the questions to be asked:

- What tools and practices do we have in place to rigorously measure our strengths, limitations, opportunities, and challenges?

- In these areas of focus, how strong are we in the tools that we use for self-regulation or organizational discipline?

- How much weight can we put on these tools (e.g., core systems) before they begin to break?
- What are our core strengths and key limitations with each of these tools?
- Are our tools better than those of our competitors or potential competitors?
- How could we leverage our core strengths in our self-regulatory tools?

The purpose of developing a comprehensive understanding of our organizational discipline is to reveal significant insights about strengths and limitations regarding capacity for growth and the kinds of risks associated with disruptive events. We are looking to evaluate how much weight the organization can bear from growth, contraction, or a variety of adverse events. It is the equivalent of making sure that our body's skeletal and muscular framework is strong. Is the organization strong enough to survive the pressures of competition? Where are we strong, and how might we leverage this? Where are we weak, and how does this make us vulnerable?

Organizational energy

The drive for results based on intrinsic values of purpose and passion is organizational energy. These values go beyond skills, status, prestige, or economic rewards. Organizational energy is enhanced through the employee experience as well as through engagement, creativity, entrepreneurism, productivity, and valuing team recognition over individual recognition. It is an expression of a healthy, dynamic, creative, problem-solving, value-creating, and humanistic culture that enables people to pursue goals with energy and persistence.

This doesn't preclude or ignore economic results, prestige, and status. Instead, it transcends these more extrinsic rewards to reach for something more purposeful—and, therefore, more fulfilling and motivating. It is the manifestation of the partnership between the individual and the organization, the alignment between individual aspirations and passions with organizational purpose. When Peter Drucker wrote, "Culture eats strategy for breakfast,"[4] he was describing an enterprise with low organizational energy.

Organizational energy is more difficult to analyze than the previous two dimensions, but it is the most critical in determining whether your strategy will be realized. The methodology and tools that we propose be used to appraise organizational energy are summarized in the following sections.

Review relevant documents

Review your company's existing documents related to the tools for measuring and amplifying energy. For example, are your HR policies focused on people and effective processes or on bureaucracy and what employees may interpret as irritating compliance requirements? How effective are your performance reviews and professional development practices? If available, review previous surveys of employee culture, engagement, or experience. You'll also want to look at HR statistics, such as retention, promotions, and so on, and observe your people in action, such as at employee celebrations or during company rituals (such as a huddle or weekly meeting).

In *Navigating the Growth Curve*,[5] James Fischer refers to this review of organizational energy as identifying the "voltage" of the organization. We are seeking to understand the currents of alignment and potential conflicting currents that will limit the organization's collective will to pursue its greatest potential. Generators of energy include enthusiasm and commitment from leaders and employees when their individual or professional aspirations are aligned with the organization's vision, values, and purpose. A spirit of collaboration among leaders and their people both within departments and across functions amplify generators of energy. The drains on energy are often recognized as individual, interpersonal, or interdepartmental conflicts of interest that cause leakage in clarity, focus, and momentum.

When Ron started working with a new client, he learned that they operated three business units that were vertically integrated. This means that the products and services of one unit served the needs of the next, which in turn, served the next. However, Ron discovered they were not relationally or operationally integrated. The leaders of the three business units never met to discuss their strengths, limitations, opportunities, challenges, or frustrations or praise for the other units. There was no discussion about optimizing the overall business, and, as a result, they always perceived a lack of support from their peers. Constant discussions took place between the business unit leaders and the CEO complaining about the other business units' failure to live up to expectations, which often went unspoken or were presented in an adversarial environment. Conflicts of interest were commonplace, and the business unit leaders cared only for their unit's targets, with little or no consideration for the needs of the other units. A constant and substantial amount of energy and time was required from the CEO to mediate these conflicts.

Ron described this lack of organizational energy as a leaky bucket. No matter how much effort the CEO put into plugging holes, a new leak would soon spring up. By getting the business unit leaders together on a regular basis to work on communication skills, negotiate for win–win relationships, and develop a greater understanding of the overarching purpose, values, and vision of the business, Ron was able to get the unit leaders to start working toward optimizing the whole. In return, the CEO could turn more of her attention to developing strategy, or, as Dr. Evans often describes it, "Creating a beautiful future together."

Interview key stakeholders

Following is a sample of the kinds of questions to be asked when interviewing key stakeholders:

EMPLOYEE ENGAGEMENT

- What level of engagement exists throughout the organization?
- Do individuals connect their own values and aspirations to those of the organization?
- Do you understand how you connect to the organization's purpose or mission?
- Do you have clear, observable actions that demonstrate living by the organization's values?
- Is there a clear understanding of how each individual's talents, skills, and passions align with their work assignments?
- How well do different departments or divisions support and communicate with each other?
- Where are bottlenecks or frustrations that steal overall motivation?
- Where is there a lack of understanding about how various functions of the organization provide value to each other and propel the goals of the organization forward?
- How well do employees identify with and demonstrate passion for customers, both internally and externally?

- What are the cultural strengths of the organization and how would you describe them?
- Where are the losses of energy in the organization, and what might be the causes for these holes in the bucket?

INDIVIDUAL PURPOSE AND FULFILLMENT
INSIDE THE ORGANIZATION

- Does the organization respect and recognize individual aspirations?
- Is there a healthy tension between individual and organizational aspirations?
- Do you feel your personal mission statement and values are given serious consideration as a vital part of the organization's commitments?
- Do your individual aspirations affect the development of organizational energy and help sustain it?
- How often do leaders ask about how your aspirations align with the organization's purpose, vision, values, and goals?
- How does this organization help you fulfill your own sense of purpose and value? What would you lose if you left the organization?

STRENGTHS AND LIMITATIONS

- What are our people's core strengths?
- With the people that we have, what can we do better than our competitors or potential competitors?

- How could we leverage our people's core strengths?
- What are our people's key limitations?
- What competencies do our people lack that limit our impact in fulfilling our purpose?
- Are there limitations that we should turn into strengths?

An organization with low energy will find it nearly impossible to reach beyond "good enough." As a leader, when there is a deficit of organizational energy, you'll spend much of your time plugging the holes and not enough time creating a beautiful future for all. Understanding and building organizational energy is about creating a culture of respect, opportunity, and enthusiasm that brings your strategy to life. Instead of culture eating strategy for breakfast, in an organization with high energy, culture makes your business come alive!

Painting a realistic picture

The questions we ask in the three dimensions should be aimed at as many key stakeholders as possible to obtain a more accurate and credible reality. This includes the board of directors, the executive team, middle management, the employees, and other stakeholders. This wide participation in contributing to the reality of an organization will reduce biases that can be associated with specific stakeholders. By so doing, we reduce the risk of basing strategy on a distorted or incomplete reality as defined by only a few stakeholders—for example, the executive team—which would bias the strategy and reduce the ownership of the rest of the stakeholders.

If your strategy doesn't take into consideration the strengths and limitations of your culture, it is doomed to fail. Culture, assumptions, values, and beliefs drive organizational behavior. They influence the way things actually get done. Culture is formed and expressed through the combination of the organization's realism, discipline, and energy.

EXTERNAL ENVIRONMENT ASSESSMENT

The two external dimensions of emotional intelligence are *social awareness*, which is the ability to understand other people's emotional makeup and how your words and actions affect them, and *social regulation*, the ability to influence the emotional clarity of others through a proficiency in managing relationships and building networks. The organizational equivalents of these dimensions are *external awareness* and *strategic partnerships*, respectively.

An assessment of this external environment requires that we identify and maintain a deep, comprehensive understanding of the organization's opportunities and challenges. It includes an exploration of problems that are also opportunities, hard and soft trends that may affect your organization, how you are perceived by those outside your organization, and how these perceptions may help or hinder the execution of strategy and the various players who are or could become customers, competitors, disruptors, or strategic partners.

External awareness

The ability to understand outside stakeholders and how their decisions and actions affect you is referred to as external awareness. This is, essentially, a focus on what is happening around your organization and identifying opportunities and challenges.[3] Another crucial aspect

---

3 Referred to as "opportunities" and "threats" in the traditional SWOT (strengths, weaknesses, opportunities, and threats) analysis.

of external awareness is how the world sees your company: your reputation and brand. Figure 2.2 provides a conceptualization of an organization's external environment, which is divided into three layers: the market environment, the competition environment, and the wider operating environment.

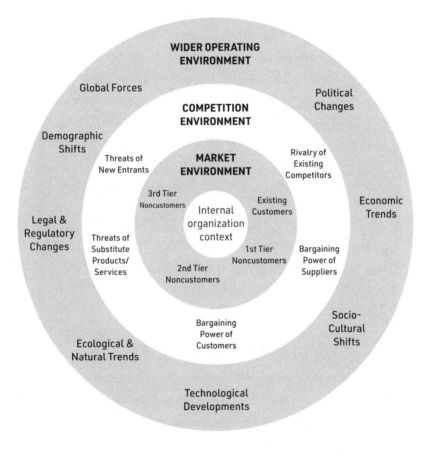

Figure 2.2. The external environment of an organization.

The market environment

Existing customers are part of an organization's market environment, which also contains three tiers of noncustomers as defined by Kim and Mauborgne.[6] First-tier noncustomers are people who minimally use the industry or organization's offerings to get by as they search for better alternatives. Kim and Mauborgne refer to them as "soon-to-be noncustomers." Second-tier noncustomers are people who either do not use or cannot use the current industry or organization's offerings because they find them unacceptable or beyond their means. Kim and Mauborgne refer to them as "refusing noncustomers." Finally, third-tier noncustomers are "unexplored noncustomers," people who have not been targeted or thought of as potential customers by any player in the industry. This may be because their needs and the business opportunities associated with them have somehow always been assumed to belong to other markets.

Most organizations will gain the greatest value by being more rigorous in understanding their existing customers. However, after mastering this understanding, organizations might find there are often hidden opportunities or challenges that are revealed through a better understanding of the three tiers of noncustomers.

It is surprising to us how often strategy is developed without first doing the rigorous work of understanding the customers' needs, challenges, interests, and experiences. Too often, leadership teams assume they understand their customers without completing the hard work of probing, listening to, and reflecting on the true voice of their customers. There are great tools and methodologies available to capture this information. However, all too often, this data is either missing from or undervalued as part of the strategy process.

Review relevant documents

The following are tools that you could use to gain strategic intelligence on customers:

- Market survey reports
- Market intelligence platforms
- Customer relations management systems analytics
- Social media systems analytics and customers' compliments or complaints
- Customer interviews and analysis

Here are some questions to ask related to customers:

- How detailed, accurate, and insightful are these various sources of customer intelligence?
- Do they provide you with an in-depth, accurate understanding of why your customers engage with you?
- Do they reveal who has quit engaging with you as a customer and why?
- Do you understand why your customers choose you over your competitors?
- Do you understand what solutions, products, or features are more or less important to your customers?
- Have your customers communicated new ways you can make your products or services more valuable to them?
- Do you have enough exposure to how your customers use your products or services to identify new opportunities that will surprise them and be useful?
- Are there opportunities for collaboration with your customers to create new products or services that will be valuable to them?

- What problems do your customers' customers have, and are there new products or services you could provide or create to increase your customers' success?

Interview key stakeholders

You'll want to interview your key internal stakeholders about customer insights. Here is a sample of the questions you could ask them about your customers:

GENERAL

- Are we clear about who our customers are?
- Do we have true voice of the customer data to guide our thinking?
- Do we have a clear definition of our ideal customer and what they want from us?
- Do we have a clear definition of who our ideal customer should be in the future and what they will want from us?
- Do we have a customer-driven understanding of how effectively we are delivering value to our customers?
- What are we exceptional at that we may be able to expand or leverage?
- Where are the gaps or challenges?
- Do we understand our existing first-tier, second-tier, and third-tier customers and what they want from us now or in the future?
- Where are the opportunities for them to become ideal customers?

OPPORTUNITIES AND CHALLENGES

- How well do we understand our customers or potential future customers?
- What data (quantitative and qualitative) do we have that is relevant, timely, and accurate?
- What are our customers' strengths and limitations, opportunities, and challenges?
- What are the strengths and limitations, opportunities, and challenges of our customers' customers?

One of the largest gaps we find over and over again in our strategy work with organizations is the lack of real, current, and insightful data from the perspective of their existing customers. Too often, leaders developing strategy have an incomplete or distorted understanding of the actual experiences of their customers. They think they understand, but they often can't communicate this in a way that gives us confidence of a deep grasp of the customer experience. This is not a book about design thinking or the customer experience, but without incorporating them as a discipline in the organization, the identification of opportunities and challenges when it comes to customers will be superficial at best. Two books we recommend for a greater mastery of customer insights are *From Voices to Results - Voice of Customer Questions, Tools, and Analysis* by Robert Coppenhaver and *Satisfaction: How Every Great Company Listens to the Voice of the Customer* by Chris Denove and James Power (from JD Power).

In reality, organizations should collect data from their customers on a continuous basis. Indeed, Verne Harnish[7] recommends that all executives and middle managers have an in-person conversation with at least one customer per week and ask the following four questions:

- How are you doing?
- What is going on in your industry or neighborhood?
- What have you heard about our competition?
- How are we doing?

This ongoing collection of data from customers is part of a continuous appraisal of the external environment that organizations must carry out as part of strategy.

The competition environment

The second layer of the external environment is the industry, or the competition environment. The factors operating in this layer are defined by Michael Porter.[8] He considers five competitive forces facing an organization: the rivalry of existing competitors, the bargaining power of your suppliers, the bargaining power of your customers or buyers, threats of new entrants to the market, and threats of substitute products or services. Following are the relevant factors Prof. Tim considers in analyzing these forces and their possible sources of data.

Rivalry between existing competitors

To assess a rivalry between existing competitors, you might interview senior strategy function managers, review sector statistics from the regulator, or commission competition intelligence reports. The relevant questions for assessing a rivalry between competitors are

- How many competitors are in our industry?
- Is there a clear market leader? Where are we vis-à-vis this leader?
- Are there high fixed costs? Can competitors cut these costs?
- How do we distinguish our products or services?

- Are there high or low switching costs?
- Are competitors pursuing aggressive growth strategies?
- Are entrance or exit barriers high or low? How does that affect the competition?

Our goal in this research is the continuous exploration to find where we may have an immediate opportunity to compete and win, or to find an eminent threat to current or new customer relationships; to search out where we might be able to displace a competitor because of greater or faster delivery of value at a lower cost; and to examine where we might be vulnerable to being displaced because of a competitor's ability to deliver greater or faster value at a lower cost. We don't have to win in all three categories, but our objective is to identify where we may have a competitive advantage. Likewise, a competitor can take business away from us without being superior in all three categories of value, timing, and cost.

When working with smaller clients, we often find them stymied when asked to identify their competitors. Identifying current and near-future competitors is not difficult; just look at your customer list over the last five years. Who did you take the business away from? Who has taken business away from you? Then look at the current advertising or social media traffic your customers are likely looking at. They often represent your competitors of the future. What might they do better than you? How might you leverage their communications to attract new customers to your business? If you don't have any competitors after these two exercises, you are fishing in blue oceans, as W. Chan Kim and Reneé put it.[9]

One fallacy we often run into is something like, "Inertia or indecision is my greatest competitor. I can't get my customers to buy!" This is an obstacle to overcome, for sure. It may be the consequence of internal

factors in your desired customers' organization, or it may be an inade-
quate understanding between you and your customers about how you
deliver value to them that is worthy of their commitment. However,
this does not fit into our analysis of competitive pressures. It belongs in
your understanding of existing customers and noncustomers.

Bargaining power of suppliers

By sifting through competition intelligence reports and interviews
with key suppliers and senior strategy function managers, you can
assess the bargaining power of your suppliers. The competition intelligence reports could come from industry or association publications,
from annual reports for relevant public companies, or from scanning
regulatory news, if your organization has a clear regulatory body. The
interviews with key suppliers and functional leaders should take place
with those you know are closest to the action of what is happening with
suppliers in your industry. Here are some relevant questions:

- Are there many customers and few dominant suppliers in
  our industry?
- Are the brands of our suppliers strong?
- Are suppliers forced to raise prices?
- Can suppliers integrate forward into the industry?
- Is it easy for suppliers to find new customers?

The purpose of this research is to identify opportunities that create leverage in your supplier relationships and to uncover challenges
that may cost you bargaining power or future access to critical supplies.
What if you learn that a major supplier has just lost a major account?
This could move you up the ladder for preferential treatment or
increased attention. What if you learn that one of your major suppliers

has just been acquired? This may present an opportunity or a challenge—or maybe even both. What if a key supplier is contemplating a direct-to-consumer model, effectively minimizing or eliminating your role? These are all examples of the opportunities and challenges you are searching for in this analysis.

Threats of substitute products or services

Interviews with key customers and senior strategy function managers can provide crucial information about threats by rival products or services that could possibly substitute for yours as a solution to a customer's need. Here are some relevant questions to ask that can assess these threats:

- Are there substitutes of better quality or lower price?
- Are customers willing to go for substitutes?
- Is it easy to switch to a substitute product or service?

Substitute products can represent a significant challenge that can shrink your market share or even put your future relevance at risk. Sometimes, substitute products grow a larger market and create future opportunities to grow your market share. Substitute services can disrupt client relationships by creating new, easier delivery methods that provide a strong competitive advantage. For example, think about the impact of Amazon's delivery service over the past 10 years. At other times, substitutes create an opportunity for you to jump on the coattails of a new service and expand your market. An example: currently, 50 percent of new book purchases and 75 percent of all e-book sales occur through Amazon. All our books—e-books and audiobooks—are now available on Amazon for a fraction of the cost it would take for us to market them outside of the Amazon ecosystem.

Bargaining power of customers

Customers also have bargaining power in their relationship with your company. To determine the level of that power, you can review market survey reports, customer relations management systems analytics, and social media systems analytics. The availability of these reports and analytics will be specific to your industry, size, and locale. Where they are available, you will usually find them via industry associations, government agencies, or consulting firms focused on customer analytics. In smaller organizations, key leaders will have a good idea of the bargaining power between the business and its customers. You'll want to ask your team these questions:

- Are there a few dominant customers and many sellers in the industry?
- Are products to customers differentiated?
- Are customers forced to be tough to be profitable?
- Is there a threat of backward and forward integration into the industry?
- Is it easy for customers to switch their suppliers?

The purpose for this research is, once again, to identify opportunities with both concentrated and diffused customer sizes and to become more aware of potential challenges, especially from current customers who may demand more value for less based on their size and volume of purchases.

Threats from new competition

Similar to the threats from new products, in the future you may face new competitors. To analyze them, you can begin by reviewing competition intelligence reports and interviews with senior strategy function managers. You'll want to ask your team the following questions:

- Are there economies of scale?
- Is our capital, or are our investment costs, high or low?
- Are the switching costs of customers high or low?
- Can new entrants access the industry's distribution channels?
- Can new entrants access and use technology to enter?
- Are our customers loyal?
- Is it likely that existing players will retaliate with new entrants?
- Can new entrants get subsidies?

Most new entrants who will be targeting your customers talk and write about it long before they actually knock on your customers' doors. However, many leaders fail to take these challenges seriously until it is too late. This was the focus of much of Clayton Christenson's work throughout his career at Harvard. His first book, *The Innovator's Dilemma*,[10] addresses this phenomenon, and most of his later writing extends this theory of creative disruption in a variety of applications. Where are you at risk of losing customers or market share because of a new entrant? What are they doing that is different? Does this represent a new opportunity for you?

The operating environment

In this ring of our concentric organizational circles, we are interested in the hard trends that will affect our organization's future, either positively or negatively. We are also interested in the soft trends that may come into play in the future. Important information can be obtained from forecasts or scenarios that others are writing or speaking about that could affect our business and execution of strategy—for example, central banks collecting data from a variety of thought leaders to inform their strategic decision-making. Ron describes one example of how he looks for and uses trends to understand the marketplace in stage 1. We wrote in stage 1, "The Foundations of Strategy," how Ron helped a food service company think 20 years into the future.

The following guidelines are used by Prof. Tim in analyzing the wider operating environment. Key factors of the wider operating environment are captured by the PESTEL (political, economic, sociocultural, technological, ecological and natural, and legal and regulatory) framework popularly used in strategic analysis. We have added two additional factors: demographic shifts and global forces.

Political changes

National or state government sector policies, political scenario analyses, and relevant political actions or decisions can be used to determine government policies and strategies, sector guidelines, and other political factors. You'll use them to guide your strategy as it relates to those factors.

Economic trends

Economic forecasts, independent economic studies, and publications from the National Statistics Office are used to determine global economic changes, GDP growth, inflation rates, taxation rates, exchange rates, employment levels, and poverty levels.

Sociocultural shifts

You can use published trends on social and cultural issues, labor trends, and publications from the National Statistics Office to examine population growth, lifestyle changes, customer preferences, labor mobility, education levels, income distribution, and governance.

Technological developments

Technological forecasts from a variety of sources can be used to analyze IT developments (e.g., artificial intelligence) and developments in relevant technologies for the industry.

Ecological and natural trends

Relevant publications from the state department in charge of the environment can be used to examine environmental factors relevant in the industry, such as conservation of the environment or climate change.

Legal and regulatory changes

New laws or changes in existing legislations and new regulations or changes by the sector regulator are crucial information about the legal framework governing the organization or the industry and regulatory requirements you'll need to abide by.

Demographic shifts

You can use the census, surveys, and publications from the National Statistics Office to determine birth and death rates, income levels, education levels, and employment and unemployment levels.

Global forces

Unexpected global changes, such as black swan events (rare and unpredictable events with potentially severe consequences) can be studied in relevant publications such as Nassim Nicholas Taleb's *Antifragile: Things That Gain from Disorder*.[11] The COVID-19 pandemic—only vaguely predictable, and globally disruptive—represents a black swan event. However, it wasn't completely unheard of, with US president George W. Bush warning of such an event during his time in office (2001–2009). Within our lifetimes, there have been many such events (e.g., the 2008 financial collapse and the 2001 terrorist attacks on the

World Trade Center in New York City and the Pentagon in Washington, DC), and there will undoubtedly be more.

Clearly, there are many avenues to explore when identifying trends that could represent opportunities or challenges to your future. From John Naisbitt's 1980s bestseller *Megatrends* to Daniel Burrus's recent blockbuster *The Anticipatory Organization*, strategy leaders are reminded to never quit scanning the horizon for new opportunities or serious threats to their business. For small organizations, active engagement with trade or industry associations will often be sufficient. Larger organizations may want to have standing committees throughout the company that are constantly monitoring publications as well as thought leaders in specific areas of focus who are regularly reporting their findings to senior management for consideration. The insights gained from this study of trends will be combined with the other opportunities and challenges of the external analysis in the next stage, strategic creative thinking.

Your reputation and brand

In addition to the layers of an organization's external environment previously described, an organization should also consider how its external stakeholders in the three layers perceive the organization. The key perceptions are about quality, value, design, social responsibility, governance, integrity, and being an employer of choice. The objective is to establish the opportunities and challenges that emanate from these perceptions. We encourage the careful assessment of both brand intention (how we want to be known in the marketplace) and brand impact (our actual reputation).

The key questions to establish those opportunities and challenges with respect to our reputation and brand are

- Which of our brand traits is strongest in the minds of our external stakeholders? What opportunities might this represent?

- How might we use this as brand currency or brand assets?
- Which of our brand traits is vulnerable in the minds of our external stakeholders?
- What challenges does this represent and how might we respond to these brand debts or liabilities?

Your brand or reputation is much like an emotional bank account. When it is strong, you have a head start in pursing new opportunities and responding to challenges. When it is weak, or focused on a narrow niche of business, you start from behind. It is valuable to understand this brand equity as you consider the other factors in your external environment. We include this as part of the external analysis because your brand is how and what outsiders think of you—not what you think of yourself. Just like every other external factor, you can use your knowledge of the opportunities and challenges around your brand to make better strategic decisions.

Strategic partnerships

The second external dimension of emotional intelligence is *social regulation,* the ability to influence others through a proficiency in managing relationships and building networks. In organizational terms, we refer to this as building strategic partnerships with customers, competitors, suppliers or vendors, regulatory bodies, and other key stakeholders.

To examine strategic partnerships in detail, we need to ask the following questions, among others:

- What are the opportunities or challenges in our current strategic partnerships?

- What makes strategic partnerships generate benefits or risks for the partners?

- What are the opportunities for new, innovative, exponentially beneficial strategic partnerships?

- How well do we understand the interests of these potential partners?

- Where do our interests and values intersect?

- Can we build a mutual belief in the potential of a strategic partnership?

- Are the potential partners able and willing to commit the necessary focus, time, and resources?

- How does diversity of perspectives, competencies, or spheres of influence make this worth pursuing?

- What potential challenges exist with these potential partners?

- Who else could be interfering with our future potential through their strategic partnership efforts apart from us?

The key to successful strategic partnerships is ensuring shared interests; shared values; mutual belief in the potential of a partnership; adequate commitment of resources; and diverse perspectives, competencies, and spheres of influence that can lead to exponential benefits.

Partnership grid

We have created a partnership grid that can help us explore the kinds of strategic partnerships we have or need to create to increase the opportunities for benefits. The partnership grid has two interacting dimensions.

The first dimension is the alignment of purpose, your *why*. The key question is the extent to which partners share beliefs or values and purpose or values and interests. When partners share the same purpose, they perceive greater value in what each other partner does. As Simon Sinek[12] argues in the context of a company and its customers, the latter will happily pay a premium or suffer some form of inconvenience to support a cause through a company if they share a *why*. When this happens, Sinek claims, the company experiences an exponential growth in their product or service. In this discussion about strategic partnerships, the partners experience exponential benefits in whatever it is they are partnering for.

The second dimension of the grid is the diversity of perspectives or ideas, competencies, and networks. The partners will bring a variety of ideas, a multiplicity of ways to execute them, and a network of relationships that create value for the partnership. This dimension represents the diversity of the *whats*, *hows*, and *whos*.

The combination of these two dimensions gives us four types of strategic partnerships: dormant, leveraged, missional, and synergistic. The outcome in each of the partnership types represents the benefits or value to the partners.

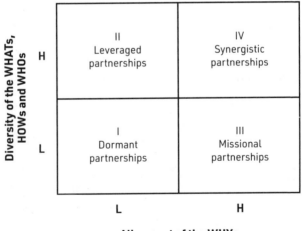

Figure 2.3: The strategic partnership grid.

Dormant partnerships

The first type (quadrant I) is what we call a dormant partnership; although the organizations have a partnership in name, they are sleeping on the potential benefits of their collaboration because of misalignments between the two partners. There is neither an alignment in beliefs nor a diversity in perspectives, competencies, and networks. The high degree of uniformity of perspectives, competencies, and networks means that the diversity of ideas, ways to implement them, and the ability to perform outreach through networks are limited. The lack of alignment in beliefs indicates that individual partners are likely to pursue and implement the common ideas with their limited networks but in line with their own beliefs, resulting in a partnership that produces mediocre benefits for the partners.

Leveraged partnerships

A leveraged partnership (quadrant II) represents a situation of low alignment in beliefs but with a high diversity in perspectives, competencies, and networks. The partners are likely to be reluctant to work together because of their poor alignment in beliefs, although there is a richness in ideas, execution of those ideas, and the networks brought on board. The individual partners are therefore likely to pay lip service to the partnership and instead pursue their own ideas and execute them with their own limited networks of relationships that are in alignment with their own values and purpose. This is likely to create chaos and limited benefits for both partners, given the pursuit of individual interests. If there are any meaningful benefits created in this partnership type, they are likely to be as a result of the influence of the more powerful members of the partnership.

We have referred to this partnership as "leveraged" because it contains the right ingredients to produce exponential benefits (diversity in perspectives, competencies, and networks) but lacks an alignment in values and purpose. In this case, *leveraged* means that we can expand our influence significantly through the combined interests, resources, and capabilities of the strategic partners.

Missional partnerships

In a missional partnership (quadrant III), the parties share their mission and purpose, but there is limited diversity in perspectives, competencies, and networks of relationships brought on board. Since there is alignment in beliefs, the partnership will achieve some benefits. However, their extent will be constrained by a lack of fertilization of many ideas, insufficient diversity in methods to implement them, and limited relationships to support the implementation.

Synergistic partnerships

In a synergistic partnership (quadrant IV), there is high diversity in perspectives, competencies, and networks of relationships brought into the partnership, and the parties are aligned in their purpose. This means that the partners can draw on and learn from varied ideas and benefit from diverse talents, which, in all likelihood, will entail some complementarity in skills and expertise. The partners also draw on the vast network of relationships brought into the partnership by the individual partners, expanding the support network of both parties. Given the high alignment in values and purpose, what the partners do and how they do it will be aligned to this common belief system. As a consequence of the richness in what, how, and who, innovation (which requires many ideas) is likely, and with the alignment in values and purpose, the potential to create a greater value for the partners is high. Given the high level of collaboration, guided by a common value system and with a common purpose, this type of partnership creates synergy. This is the only type of strategic partnership that is likely to experience exponential benefits for the partners.

We must caution, however, that it is not automatic that even a synergistic partnership will realize exponential value. Challenges may affect this realization. It may be aided or hindered by the mechanisms that allow partners to contribute their ideas, skills, and expertise; the transparency and openness of processes; and the effectiveness of communication. Successful strategic partnerships are characterized by high levels of trust and commitment, effective communication, managed power imbalances between the partners, increased participation by both parties, and effective mechanisms of conflict resolution.[13] However, the alignment of the partners' values and purpose reduces these challenges and their effects.

STAKEHOLDER ANALYSIS

It is important to analyze the stakeholders of an organization to determine how they could affect the strategy process. One of the tools Prof. Tim has used extensively for this analysis is the interest-influence grid. It maps stakeholders according to their interest and power or influence.

The influence dimension represents the extent to which the stakeholder can persuade or coerce others into making decisions and following certain courses of action. Those with high influence are likely to be your most useful supporters or most dangerous opponents.

The interest dimension represents the level of interest the stakeholder has in your strategy. This is likely to be most obvious when stakeholder interests converge closely with those of your business.

Figure 2.4 illustrates the interest-influence grid. This analysis helps us prioritize the top five stakeholders whose interests we most need to pay attention to.

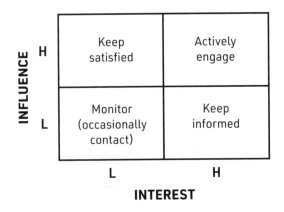

Figure 2.4. The interest-influence grid.

Low interest-low influence

Low interest-low influence stakeholders are relatively unimportant to the success of your business. You only need to keep in touch with them in case their status changes.

High interest-low influence

High interest-low influence stakeholders only need to be informed because they may gain influence by low-level blocking—for example, if they resist the strategy.

Low interest-high influence

Low interest-high influence stakeholders will not be worried about what you do but can derail the strategy if they are persuaded to act by those opposed to the strategy. Therefore, you must keep them satisfied.

High interest-high influence

High interest-high influence stakeholders are key players who will be significantly affected by the strategy and who have the influence to do something about it—either by supporting or opposing the strategy. It is important to actively engage these stakeholders in your strategy, ensuring that they understand and buy into it.

SLOC ANALYSIS

We use the strengths, limitations, opportunities, and challenges (SLOC) analysis as a way to summarize the strategic intelligence gathered in stage 2. In general, we wish to seize the opportunities identified, avoid the challenges that pose the highest risk to the organization's success, maximize the use of our strengths, and minimize the impact of our limitations. To summarize the vast amount of strategic intelligence gathered with the tools provided in this chapter into a SLOC summary framework as shown in figure 2.5, we recommend the following set of actions:

- Identify all distinctive competencies (strengths), key limitations, strategic opportunities, and key challenges.

- Eliminate all operational strengths, limitations, opportunities, or challenges; operational items are those with limited impact, are short-term oriented, are detailed, and can be sorted out in routine operational management.

- Insert the output into the SLOC framework shown in figure 2.5, focusing only on the top five to nine SLOC elements under each category. Your strategy will be developed around these SLOC elements.

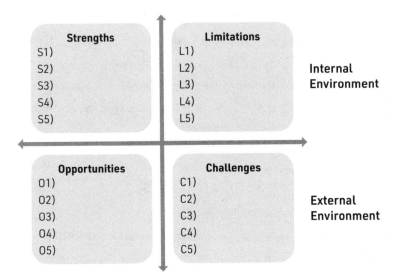

Figure 2.5. SLOC summary framework.

The internal and external environmental assessments, which, in traditional strategy work, constitute the analytical effort to understand where an organization is, create a strong basis for developing a strategy. This basis needs to be packaged into a coherent *why* for strategy development and communicated effectively across all key stakeholders in the organization. This communication will encourage participation in the strategy process. Specifically, the communication should help the key stakeholders personalize the challenges and limitations the organization faces and catapult them into thinking about how they can assist in getting out of the current reality. The communication here should act to reinforce the purpose established in stage 1.

One of our global clients collected insights for their SLOC analysis by asking all their locations around the world to complete a SLOC exercise for their specific spheres of influence. The data was collected, organized, and analyzed by a broad strategic planning group to identify the commonality and potential impact of the identified issues. By collecting this information from the bottom up, the planners were able to develop strategic themes that were relevant and compelling across the entire organization.

TAKING ACTION

Everyone in an organization can and should learn how to identify the company's internal strengths and limitations and contribute to an understanding of external opportunities and challenges. This should not be an annual event but a yearlong exercise in strategic intelligence that results in the entire organization preparing for better strategic decisions.

WHY

The quantity and quality of analysis in this stage is crucial to developing informed strategic options. The internal analysis helps identify the organization's capacities for successfully executing strategy. The external analysis helps identify what opportunities and challenges will inform the significance of strategic options.

WHAT

Data and insights should flow from the bottom up in the organization. Employees, their supervisors, and other middle managers are often keenly aware of the strengths and limitations around the organization's realism, discipline, and energy. Those people closest to the customers will often be aware of opportunities or challenges that deserve careful consideration. Market research experts (internal or external) should have detailed analysis of the five competitive forces. Your organization should also have groups of subject matter experts or utilize think tanks experienced and always current in their understanding of hard and soft trends that will represent future opportunities or challenges. After collecting the data and insights flowing up the organization, those responsible for establishing strategic themes should communicate their decisions and link them back to the upward flow of information, both to reinforce the value of this data collection and to build commitment to future strategic themes.

WHEN

Strategic intelligence continues to grow and improve when the collection of data and insights is continuous, with reporting to senior leaders taking place based on the rhythms of strategic planning, execution, and evaluation. For most organizations, this means there should be substantive reports with new data or insights provided to senior leadership no less than quarterly. Updates from senior leadership to the employee population should take place as often as necessary to continue building momentum around the seven stages of strategy and optimizing strategy results.

WHO

It is important for people throughout the organization to understand the significance of providing insights around the internal strengths and limitations, as well as the external opportunities and challenges, that may inform, amplify, or hinder the pursuit of the purpose and vision of the organization.

HOW

Research, stakeholder conversations, industry and sector briefings, internal surveys, and analysis are all vital parts of developing substantive strategic intelligence. The goal should be to provide the best insights possible, in a timely manner, to those developing strategic options and themes.

KEY TAKEAWAYS

TOOLS

In this chapter, we covered the methodology and tools to analyze

- Organizational awareness
- Organizational discipline
- Organizational energy
- Customers
- Competitive forces
- Hard and soft trends
- The influence (or hindrance) of reputation
- Strategic partnerships

PEOPLE

- As many individuals as possible who are keenly aware of the internal and external factors

- People who are keenly aware of the interests of the key stakeholders
- People with strong skills in futuristic thinking, conceptual thinking, creativity, continuous learning, and customer focus

RESULTS

- SLOC summary

PART 2

CREATING STRATEGY

Skills to succeed: creativity, futuristic thinking,
conceptual thinking, persuasion, negotiation,
decision-making, planning and organizing

STAGE 3

— ▲ —

CREATIVE STRATEGIC THINKING

Our third stage, creative strategic thinking, involves creatively generating options from the strategic intelligence gathered in stage 2. Organizations need to know what options are available to them. These options answer two key questions: Where do you need to be in the future, and how do you get there? The options should, therefore, be able to provide the best outcomes that make the most use of your strengths, seize available opportunities, avoid challenges (or convert them into opportunities), and minimize the impact of the limitations (or convert them into strengths).

Figure 3.1 shows the three main processes that take place in stage 3.

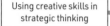

Figure 3.1. Stage 3 processes.

USING CREATIVE SKILLS IN STRATEGIC THINKING

When generating options that will provide a competitive advantage, it is important to tap into your team's creativity, which will increase the chances of getting transformative options. In strategy development, there is often an overemphasis on the use of analytical tools such as SWOT, five forces, and competitive analysis (all covered in the previous chapter). Although these tools are important in strategy development and implementation, utilizing them may often lead to the development of conventional boilerplate strategies that lack imagination or futuristic views and that are often reactive to the past or current environment.

Effective plans, choices, and decisions that are the cornerstone of a great strategy are built on the foundation of varied ideas. These ideas provide the raw materials for building a breakthrough strategy, but the ideas must be sourced by engaging stakeholders and conducting specific exercises that result in multiple options. In fact, a large quantity of ideas must be a priority at this stage—the more the ideas, the better. Sources, methods of idea generation, and even methods of evaluation require a process of creativity.[1] Therefore, creativity is at the center of any good strategy development and cannot be underestimated.

Effective creative exercises involve the complex integration of emotions and reasoning. As a leader, you must engage both sides of human faculties and be comfortable with the ideas necessary to mine deeper levels of creativity. Leading your organization through a strategic creative thinking exercise involves three phases: preparing the creative exercises, conducting the creative exercises, and analyzing the data from the creative exercises.

Preparing creative exercises

The best thinking is intentional, aimed at a specific purpose, and open to different kinds of ideas. No idea is bad or great at this point, but all are valid. The goal is to get the idea factories—human brains—running.

To help get the most ideas from your stakeholders, start by breaking down subject areas into smaller sections. For example, break marketing into individual segments such as products, positioning, internal communications, external communications, promotion, and so on. This allows you to ask specific questions and get the most ideas collectively on all important areas from various stakeholders.

Next, generate questions that you need answered by your stakeholders. They are the foundation of the creativity exercises. Here are a few examples:

- What problems do we want to solve?
- Who are our customers?
- Do we need to change or modify our offerings?
- Do we need new or different customers?
- What do we want to be known for in the marketplace?
- Where will the organization's financial position be in X years?
- What do you see as your contribution to that future state?

Finally, create guidelines for your idea generation team. Following are the nine key ground rules for effective idea generation:

- Use probing, stimulating questions.
- Challenge assumptions.
- Listen to your customers.
- Generate ideas that benefit the customers.
- Engage your stakeholders.
- Establish an open and blame-free environment.
- Encourage risk taking (as opposed to risk management).
- Avoid acceptance of the status quo.
- Don't prejudge ideas; all ideas get recorded.

Conducting creative exercises

When you invite stakeholders to help generate ideas, you must emotionally engage them. The goal is to keep asking questions. You can start with a simple question and keep asking *why* or *what else* or *what if*. This encourages deeper and wider thinking. In addition, it allows your stakeholders to generate and submit ideas in different forms (written, short form, long form, descriptive, illustrations, and pictures) and in different formats (electronic, physical, verbal).

The goal is to get as many ideas as possible. Whenever your stakeholders generate and provide ideas, it is important to celebrate their contributions through timely acknowledgment.

Prof. Tim worked with a team of 20 managers in a public enterprise in Kenya. One of our organizational assessments indicated a low level of creative thinking, so Prof. Tim led the managers in a new way to create strategic options. Each manager was asked to write down, on Post-it notes, three problems that needed to be resolved. They were added to the previously completed SLOC analysis. The managers generated more than 60 problems. They were then challenged to identify three different ways to solve each problem, resulting in close to 200 additional strategic options to be considered.

Next, Prof. Tim asked the managers to place each of their problem Post-it notes, along with the attendant strategic options, on the wall. The problems were written on one color of Post-it notes and the strategic options in another. The managers then arranged the problems and strategic options according to strategic themes. Ten major themes emerged, which Prof. Tim determined was too many for the group's capacities. He asked each of the managers to rank or prioritize the themes from most important to least important, and, after tallying the results, the managers agreed to focus on the top seven options. They then went through the same process, identifying the top five to seven strategic options under each strategic theme. The managers were energized by this process and convinced they had identified the strategic options that mattered most.

Analyzing the data

Once you have collected the ideas, the work of evaluating and creating options begins. First, organize the ideas based on categories, subjects, and subsections. Then, start the work of evaluating the ideas based on how much value they have, not necessarily by how good they are. Some ideas may seem irrelevant at first, but continuous evaluation can result in improvement. Continuous evaluation involves eight activities represented by the acronym SCAMPER[2]:

- Substitute
- Combine
- Add
- Modify or magnify
- Put to other use
- Eliminate
- Rearrange or reverse

SCAMPERing helps not only in idea evaluation but also in further ideation. Ideas are always regenerating into greater value when they are evaluated through this process. After SCAMPERing, according to Adam Brandenburger,[3] create options by implementing the four Cs: contrast ideas, combine ideas, convert constraints into strengths, and contextualize by learning how a similar problem is being solved in other circumstances.

Contrast

Identify the assumptions implicit in the existing strategies that undergird the status quo. This allows the strategy team to identify opportunities to reinvent a business. For example, if the business is based in a physical location, where customers come for the product, what would happen if the product were delivered to the customers instead? Would it be faster, cheaper, or more convenient for both buyers and sellers? Create options by identifying ways to deliberately disturb an aspect of your normal patterns to break up ingrained assumptions.

Combine

Identify opportunities that combine products or services that are currently independent or in opposition with one another to create new offerings. This may combine services or products that have traditionally been separated into new value chains. For example, taking a mobile phone service and integrating it with a money transfer and payment service, which was the case of Mpesa in Kenya (owned by Safaricom) and WeChat Pay in China (owned by Tencent). Now you can create options by forming groups with diverse expertise and experience and challenging them to brainstorm new combinations of products and services. Another way is to coordinate with providers of complementary products (who may even be competitors).

Convert

Identify organizational limitations and consider how they might actually become strengths. This applies to both market-imposed and self-imposed constraints. In strategic creative thinking, a constraint is not something to run away from but an opportunity to use your imagination, eventually helping the company turn it into a strength. For example, Tesla did not have a traditional dealer network for their electric vehicles, so they used a constraint to create an online sales methodology, controlling pricing and creating deeper relationships directly with their car buyers. To create options, list the "incompetencies" (rather than the competencies) of your organization and test whether they can, in fact, be turned into strengths.

Contextualize

Identify how a problem similar to yours is being solved in a different context or industry. This information will become a source of insight and knowledge transfer. For example, when dealing with a complex problem in engineering, such as aerodynamics, engineers would spend time with biologists or zoologists learning how birds of varying sizes and shapes are able to navigate different natural forces while flying. Out of such interactions, the engineers gain deeper knowledge about how to balance weight, reduce friction, and increase acceleration, among other topics. Similar collaboration happens between electrical chip designers and pharmaceutical chemists when exploring complex chemical architecture. To create options, identify your business challenges and explain them to an outsider in another industry or context. Discuss their points of view and try to uncover new answers and opportunities.

GENERATING STRATEGIC OPTIONS

The procedure previously described will help you generate many options. It is critical that you have as many options as possible; you want to be spoiled for choice rather than forced to choose fairly obvious strategies that have become familiar over time.

The following framework can help you generate even more options. It starts with the four SLOC questions shown in table 3.1, which are based on the SLOC summary generated in stage 2 (figure 2.5).

Table 3.1. SLOC questions		
	Strengths	**Limitations**
Opportunities	How will we use our strengths to take advantage of the opportunities?	How will we tackle our limitations to prevent ourselves from missing opportunities?
Challenges	How will we use our strengths to reduce probability and impact of the challenges?	How will we act on our limitations to mitigate the challenges?

We can use the questions in table 3.1 to create all possible SLOC combinations and generate their attendant options as the answers to these questions. In generating the options, we can use the ground rules proposed earlier, including challenging the assumptions and status quo, generating ideas that benefit customers, establishing an open and blame-free environment, and encouraging risk taking. The following examples illustrate how to generate options that represent answers to each of the key questions in table 3.1.

When Ron facilitates the development and prioritizing of strategic options, he first breaks the strategy team into four groups. One group discusses and narrows down the list of internal strengths; the second group, the list of internal limitations; the third group, the list of external opportunities; and the fourth group, the list of external challenges. Once these lists have been winnowed down to the five most significant in each category, Ron reorganizes the groups, beginning with half of each group that had been working on either strengths or opportunities.

This new group compares and contrasts potential options by reviewing the two lists (strengths and opportunities). Then he takes the other half of the strengths group and assigns them with half of the challenges group to compare and contrast the potential options on these two lists (strengths and challenges). Ron then assigns half of the limitations group with half of the opportunities group (limitations and opportunities) and the other half of the limitations group with the other half of the challenges group (limitations and challenges) to do the same thing—compare and contrast the potential options. During this exercise, Ron asks the four groups to develop as many options as possible within a prescribed period of time determined by the size of the groups, the rhythm of strategy development in the organization, and so on. His target is for them to develop 100 or more options in a creative, non-judgmental way.

Once the creative thinking portion of ideation is completed, Ron asks the four groups to establish a criterion for evaluating the options and to begin pairing down the number of options in preparation for making strategic decisions, as explained in stage 4. The questions each group addresses are described in the following examples.

How will we use our strengths to take advantage of opportunities?

Let us consider one strength and one opportunity in answering this question. For example:

- Strength #1 from our SLOC analysis: a large customer base for our flagship products or services

- Opportunity #1 from our SLOC analysis: new markets in other countries

From these two SLOC elements, we can generate the following options:

- Option #1: These abilities allow us to improve the quality of our customer service to enhance existing customer retention.
- Option #2: To retain existing customers, we can offer complimentary products or services.
- Option #3: We can also market products and services and seek partnerships to enter into new markets.

How will we tackle our limitations to prevent from missing opportunities?

A limitation made clear by this question may be that we lack experience in data analytics related to the work of our customers. An opportunity in this area may perhaps be a strong trend toward using analytics in decision-making for a major customer. The available options in this case would be

- #1: To partner with a data analytics firm that doesn't currently work in our customers' industry
- #2: To develop a data analytics department and build it as a new competency in our business
- #3: To partner with our major customer to jointly develop data analytics resources, tools, and competencies that we end up co-owning
- #4: To partner with several regional competitors to develop data analytics as a new competency that we can all use in our respective markets

How will we use our strengths to reduce probability and the impact of the challenges?

Our strength in this case could be that we have assets, land, and expertise in growing, processing, and selling carrots. The challenge might be that the carrot market is oversupplied and consumption is decreasing (excessive supply–decreasing demand). Options include

- #1: We could look for other another crop to grow and could process and sell it using our current assets, land, and expertise.
- #2: We could look for opportunities to consolidate with other carrot growers to gain more leverage in the supply arena.
- #3: We could expand our sales and distribution activities to cover larger geographical areas.
- #4: We could develop new uses for carrots as foodstuffs and supplement nutrients in partnership with universities and also develop nonfood uses.

How will we act on our limitations to mitigate the challenges?

Our limitation in this case might be a noninnovative culture, which creates the challenge of declining sector or industry performance in combination with the COVID-19 pandemic. Our options include

- #1: Reforming the organizational processes to enhance agility and improve organizational performance
- #2: Engaging customers to establish how we can help them cope with the effects of the COVID-19 pandemic

- #3: Reviewing our business strategy to factor in the effects of the COVID-19 pandemic and reposition the organization

Given a minimum of three and a maximum of seven elements in each SLOC perspective, there will be a minimum of 36 and a maximum of 196 SLOC combinations, respectively. If we assume a minimum of two and a maximum of three strategic options for each SLOC combination, there will be 72 and 588 strategic options, respectively, for a minimum of three and a maximum of seven elements in each SLOC perspective.

We can generate more than three options for each SLOC combination, depending on how we engage the strategic planning teams. We can, for example, use the creative methods previously outlined to increase the number of options we create. This is effectively accomplished by emotionally engaging the strategic planning stakeholders at each SLOC combination and repeatedly asking *why*, *what else*, or *what if* questions.

While working with a leading global technology company based in Silicon Valley, one of the challenges Dr. Evans faced was how to continually grow market share in various internal markets for the products and services from R&D. The global market share was more than 60 percent, worth more than $4 billion in average annual revenue. Some of the key insights (problem–opportunities) from the strategic intelligence were that each market was different: Each of the key customers had a different set of needs and areas of focus. Some of the customers were competitors, even across borders, but they wanted exclusivity of services in certain jurisdictions. The periods to realize revenue targets also varied for the different markets, trading cycles were different by markets, and competitors were also courting the same customers.

As part of the options-creating sessions, Dr. Evans first tackled each of the problem–opportunities individually. How can we turn each of these insights into a strength? How about making it a larger opportunity? How can we address the limitations and eliminate as many constraints as possible? This exercise took many hours and sessions, with each participant contributing their thoughts. Then the four Cs approach was implemented to help expand and contrast ideas. This exercise yielded about 512 ideas (options) that cut across multiple problem–opportunities, which were later filtered down during the decision-making process.

TAKING ACTION

It takes a large quantity of ideas to create a great strategy. The collection and management of ideas is when everyone can contribute. There is a proven structure for collecting, processing, and evaluating ideas that will lead to better decision-making around strategic themes.

WHY

Creative strategic thinking opens up possibilities for significant breakthroughs and innovations in the development of strategic options. Because everyone in your organization has the ability to contribute ideas, it is important to encourage, collect, and evaluate these ideas over time (not just as a one-time event). Position, experience, and expertise are not guarantees of creative strategic thinking. Therefore, the broader the audience that you engage as idea generators, the greater the chance you will discover new strategic options for fulfilling your purpose and vision.

WHAT

After summarizing the pertinent aspects of strategic intelligence, it is valuable to engage a large number of stakeholders in generating strategic options. These options should then be organized topically and further developed using SCAMPER and the four Cs. The more people you teach how to use these methods in generating and refining ideas, the greater the number of ideas you will have to consider as strategic options.

WHEN

Although creative strategic thinking can and should take place year-round, the most important period to focus on this is up to 60 days prior to identifying strategic themes.

WHO

In a culture of innovation, everyone is a contributor. This includes employees, customers, suppliers, employee family members, and so on. Communicating and reinforcing the culture with all stakeholders throughout the year will feed the ongoing creative thinking process.

HOW

Set up idea banks to collect and sort ideas. Schedule idea-generation meetings with diverse groups of stakeholders. Assign topical lists of ideas to different groups for the development of strategic options. Identify idea champions who enjoy creating quantities out of ideas, evaluating ideas, SCAMPERing, and using the four Cs method.

Finally, by using SLOC analysis, assign specific groups to generate strategic options.

KEY TAKEAWAYS

TOOLS

- Creative exercises to generate ideas
- SCAMPER and the four Cs framework to evaluate ideas
- SLOC analysis framework to generate strategic options

PEOPLE

- Several groups of three to seven people will generate more ideas than fewer groups or larger groups.
- Diverse perspectives, skills, and networks will generate more options.
- Creative thinking, problem-solving, and futuristic thinking skills will generate more and better options.

RESULTS

- Strategic options

STAGE 4

— ▲ —

MAKING STRATEGIC DECISIONS

From the options generated in stage 3, we need to filter out the best ones based on our capabilities (strengths and limitations), as well as external opportunities and challenges that we have identified. We have to bear in mind that not all options can be implemented—for example, due to a lack of resources or because they are not acceptable to some key stakeholders. The alternatives must therefore be evaluated using multiple criteria, including their consistency with the organization's long-term vision and purpose, available resources, and their possible contribution to the organization's ultimate value creation. We must then group these selected options using themes, which we'll subsequently identify as either strategic or tactical. Finally, we'll develop specific goals and objectives for our strategy. A summary of the stage 4 processes is summarized in figure 4.1.

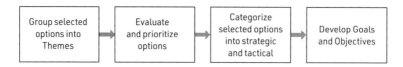

Figure 4.1. Stage 4 processes.

CREATING
STRATEGIC THEMES

Before you evaluate your options, you need to create strategic themes. Themes are structural boundaries to place around your options, or buckets to put your options in. These themes help create clarity and placement for each option.

Strategic themes are the strategic focus areas for the business around which strategy is developed and implemented. They emerge from the options generated in stage 3. These themes are obtained by grouping all related options into a distinct set. For example, options related to people are grouped under a strategic theme called "people." Grouping helps us allocate responsibility for specific aspects of the strategy and for specific functional units of the organization during strategy execution. For example, all the outcomes, key performance indicators, and targets relating to the theme "people" would be allocated to the functional unit in charge of those issues.

Key roles of strategic themes focus our organizational attention— resource allocation, decision-making, and prioritization, among other factors—on what is really important. They also represent issues that the organization needs to address expeditiously and effectively for the business to thrive. Subsequently, they become the basis for developing the rest of the strategy outputs, including goals, objectives, and initiatives.

Ideally, you should have only a few themes. In our practice, we have found that five to seven are appropriate. If more than seven themes are created, it might be an indication that some of them, including their options, are not a priority. We have also observed that the greater the number of themes, the greater the risk of failing to achieve superior performance in each.

EVALUATE AND PRIORITIZE OPTIONS

There are many methods we can use to evaluate the options discovered in the previous stage. For example, we can use the SLOC framework to assess the suitability of an option in terms of the extent to which it addresses the strengths, limitations, opportunities, and challenges relating to the strategic position of the organization. However, because we used SLOC in stage 3, it would not be suitable to use it again at this stage, so let's look at alternatives. The goal is to improve and organize the options so they can easily be evaluated and prioritized. There are multiple ways to evaluate your options, each with strengths, limitations, and—ultimately—suitability based on your organizational context and experience. To get started, we introduce two simple methods: the ABCD prioritization method and the resource–return grid.

ABCD prioritization

We have successfully used the popular ABCD prioritization method to label options for our own organizations and clients. Each option would first be assigned a letter according to the following parameters:

- A: Options that are vital to survival as an organization.
- B: Options that are not critical to survival but appear to be important for success.
- C: Options that have some but not primary importance.
- D: Options that have unknown or no importance.

After sorting the themes and options into these four categories, the options labeled A are then prioritized numerically, with the most critical being labeled A1, then A2, and so on. Our experience has shown that the only options that move to the next phase of consideration are those labeled A or B, and even then, several of the B options are often set aside at this point.

This is how Dr. Evans used the ABCD model with his Silicon Valley client after categorizing the ideas into three strategic themes. The themes were market share growth (revenue), intellectual property partnerships (expanding the R&D base and adaption of new and future products and services), and people (the ability to attract and retain top national and regional talent).

In step 1, each of the 512 options were assigned to one of the three strategic themes. In this case, there were 190 options on revenue, 314 options on intellectual property, and 8 ideas on talent.

In step 2, the options for each of the themes were then filtered following the ABCD method. The output of that exercise is laid out in table 4.1.

Table 4.1. ABCD method example			
ABCD method	**Market share**	**Intellectual property**	**People**
A. Options that are vital to survival as an organization	79	8	5
B. Options that are not critical to survival but appear to be important for success	67	197	1
C. Options that have some but not primary importance	6	38	2
D. Options that have unknown or no importance*	38	71	1
Total	190	314	8

*One of the reasons for the many options in D is that they may not be large or significant enough to be standalone options. They could be integrated into objectives or tactics or could be further combined with other options. We encourage our clients to go through this exercise for all classifications in each theme.

Step 3 focuses on class A items in each of the themes and filters further for value. In fact, you can use the four Cs method again to try to narrow down and strengthen the options. In our case, for example, we used the four Cs to convert the 79 market share A options into nine very strong options. We recommend that you repeat the same for each of your strategic themes to produce a manageable list of stronger options. Whenever possible, have fewer than 10 options for each strategic theme in the A class. The fewer A options, the easier the decision-making. If you don't identify enough options in the A category, you can always dip into the B category of options.

Step 4 is to take the options identified in B, C, and D and store them in your idea bank for future review. You can incorporate them into the A options later in the process or review them in future planning sessions.

The resource–return grid

Another method that can be used to prioritize options to be implemented is the resource–return grid shown in figure 4.2. Resources include the sum of time, money, and expertise, whereas returns include financial, experience, and innovation factors. Because there may be too many options for the organization to execute well, those in the "priority" and "important" quadrants are selected.

Similar to the ABCD method, you should start by creating themes and assigning your options into them. Going back to Dr. Evan's example of working with a company in Silicon Valley, there were three strategic themes: market share growth (revenue), intellectual property partnerships (expanding the R&D base and adoption of new and future products and services), and people (the ability to attract and retain top national and regional talent).

Step 1 was to assign each of the 512 options into each of the three strategic themes. In this case, there were 190 options for revenue, 314 options for intellectual property, and 8 ideas for talent.

Step 2 was to classify the options by placing them in different parts of the resource–return grid. Next, produce three different schematics for each of the themes. Following is an example of options for the market share theme.

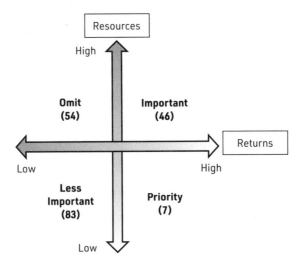

Figure 4.2. Resource–return grid for the market share theme.

Step 3 was to focus on understanding the assumptions and justification of the priority and important options in each theme.

Finally, step 4 was similar to the ABCD model: The "important" and "less important" options should be placed in your idea bank or used to strengthen your priority options.

Because of the complexity of the organization Dr. Evans was working with, and because each of the themes related to countries and markets needed further refinement for these themes to best match their context, more than one prioritization method was needed. In this instance, they combined the ABCD prioritization method with the resource–return grid. In this example, in step 1 they completed the ABCD prioritization method. In step 2, they removed the output of the ABCD method, focusing on the A and B options, taking them through the resource–return grid method. Dr. Evans found this amazingly effective, and it led to easy decisions.

Let's take the example of market share theme. From ABCD we have group A: options that are vital to survival as an organization (79), and group B: options that are not critical to survival but appear to be important for success (67). When we took these options (a total of 146) through the resource–return grid, the results were those shown in figure 4.3.

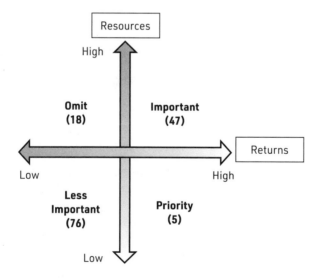

Figure 4.3. Resource–return grid based on the ABCD results f
or the market share theme.

As you can see, the number of options that are crucial for the organization is now five—a lot more manageable.

When using the combined approach, we recommend that you compare A options from the ABCD method and the priority options under the resource–return grid for a combined approach. This helps validate whether you would have reached the same conclusions and whether there are differences, as well as identifies those differences and why they appear.

We prefer combining these two approaches, using both the ABCD prioritization framework and the resource–return grid. For example, the options in the "priority" quadrant in the grid would be the priority A options. In this case, these options would then be prioritized numerically, with the most critical being labeled A1, then A2, and so on. This allows us to select the "high priority" and "important" options but also to prioritize within those groups so that we can quickly see the highest priority and most important options.

The SAFe-A method

A multiple-criteria framework that prioritizes options is a third approach that Prof. Tim has used to great success. This is a quantitative, formal evaluation framework that assesses the options utilizing four main criteria: suitability, acceptability, feasibility, and alignment, which we abbreviate as SAFe-A.

Suitability

Suitability examines the extent to which a strategic option fits with the key organizational drivers, fits with expected changes in both the internal and external environments, exploits organizational strategic capabilities, is appropriate in the context of stakeholder expectations and influence, and is appropriate in terms of cultural influence.

Acceptability

Acceptability entails expected performance outcomes of a strategic option in terms of return, risk, and stakeholder acceptability. Return includes both financial and nonfinancial benefits that stakeholders are expected to receive from a strategic option, such as a return on capital employed, a cost–benefit analysis, and a payback period for financial benefits. The risk associated with this criterion includes the probability and consequences of the failure of a strategic option, such as adverse changes in capital structure and liquidity position. Stakeholder acceptability is the likelihood of acceptance of a strategic option by your company's stakeholders.

Feasibility

Feasibility is whether an organization has the resources and competencies to deliver a strategy in terms of financial feasibility, the availability of resources and competencies, organizational feasibility, the ability to meet critical success factors, and the ability to create and sustain a competitive advantage.

Alignment

Alignment is the extent to which a strategic option is aligned to the strategy execution time frame (e.g., three years or five years), the long-term vision, the purpose, and the core values of your organization.

We typically go further in practice and use these four criteria and their subcriteria in a color-coded chart, which makes it easier to quickly visualize the best options, but the concept is the same.

In table 4.2, we give an example of a financial technology start-up company evaluating a set of four strategic options in its diversification strategy using the SAFe-A framework. For illustrative purposes, the four options were rated by three people on a scale of 1 to 10 on each of the four evaluation criteria, with the average calculated. Option 2 followed by option 1 seemed to be the best evaluated. The company may choose to pursue both options.

Table 4.2. Example of using the SAFe-A evaluation framework																	
Strategic option	**Suitability**				**Acceptability**				**Feasibility**				**Alignment**				**Overall Avg**
	P1	**P2**	**P3**	**Avg**	**P1**	**P2**	**P3**	**Avg**	**P1**	**P2**	**P3**	**Avg**	**P1**	**P2**	**P3**	**Avg**	
Introduce new products in existing market segments	5	6	4	5	7	6	8	7	10	9	8	9	9	10	8	9	7.5
Introduce existing products in new market segments	9	8	10	9	10	10	10	10	10	9	8	9	9	9	9	9	9.3
Introduce new products in new market segments	4	3	2	3	4	3	2	3	6	7	8	7	6	5	4	5	4.5
Acquire existing FinTech companies with their products in eight new regional markets as a faster way of entering these markets	6	7	8	7	5	4	6	5	3	4	2	3	2	3	1	2	4.3

STRATEGIC VERSUS TACTICAL

Some selected options will be strategic, others tactical. There is often confusion regarding the difference between these complementary categories. The organization must have both elements to be successful, and you must know the difference.

Strategic options represent the long-term and broad pathway that will help the organization achieve its vision. From them, we derive the long-term goals and objectives of the company.

Tactical options, on the other hand, are short-term actions that require smaller steps to move you toward your vision. Your tactical options will become execution elements in stage 6 of our strategy process.

Figure 4.4 shows how each piece fits together.

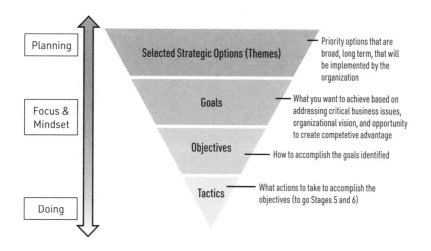

Figure 4.4. The elements of strategy.

Within each theme, we categorize the options into strategic (long-term) and tactical (short-term) options, as shown in the following example. The strategic options will be used in the next subsection to develop goals and objectives, and the tactical options will be used in the more detailed planning and execution stages (stages 5 and 6, respectively).

Strategic and tactical options

THEME 1: MARKET SHARE (REVENUE)

Strategic options

- New product
- New long-term R&D partner

Tactical Options

- Increase promotional events
- Lower price by X percent this year

Tactical elements are implemented to influence the success or failure of the business goal in its current state. They are always defined in the context of the current environment and latest data and are executed while that context is still present. These are specific actions needed to achieve goals, now. If the context changes, the tactics must also change. Goals and objectives (strategic options), on the other hand, are evergreen. They dictate the types of tactics that will be appropriate for a given context, but it does not change with that context. Tactical elements are measured reactively, whereas goals and objectives success can only be measured over time, based on the accumulation of tactical data.

GOALS AND OBJECTIVES

A goal is a broad statement about where the organization wants to be over the plan period. It puts strategic focus into the organization, addresses all strategic options in the theme, and must support the purpose and vision of the organization in the context of its core values. We have found it useful to develop one goal for each theme. In some exceptional circumstances, a theme may have more than one goal. For instance, if we continue our previous example, the goal for the company would be to increase market share in the United States to 45 percent.

Objectives[4] describe how to achieve the defined goals, and their measurement takes place in the future. There are, however, many ways of achieving a goal. Therefore, it's important to generate as many potential objectives as possible and then use a set of criteria to evaluate and select the ones to pursue (e.g., increase market share in the United States to 45 percent in the next 36 months, or recruit two new research partners in Southeast Asia in the next 24 months).

Goals and objectives are strategic; they do not necessarily change as a result of a change of context. They are not defined by your tactical choices; rather, your goals define your objectives, which, in turn, inform your tactical decisions. For example, the goal could be to grow market share. The objective may be low-price positioning, and the tactics could be low-price promotions and/or time-bound giveaways. These tactics can be employed one at a time or simultaneously, depending on factors such as customer or competition responses. Measuring the success of any given tactic is less important than measuring the success of the objective.

Goals, objectives, and tactics form a hierarchy, as is shown in figure 4.5. It takes multiple goals to deliver the overall strategy and several objectives to deliver a goal. Similarly, it takes many and different tactics to deliver an objective that eventually delivers the goal. In fact, some

---

4   In some literature and practice, these are referred to as *strategies*. In this book, we refer to them as objectives so that we can reserve the use of the term "strategy" to refer to the totality—as in strategy development and strategy execution.

tactics may not seem related to the objective because they may be the building blocks of another tactic, with multiple layers removed from the actual objective. It is therefore important to ensure that everyone in your organization understands how their tactical work, cumulatively, affects the overall objectives and goals. Eventually, this communication and collaboration will determine your strategy's success or failure.

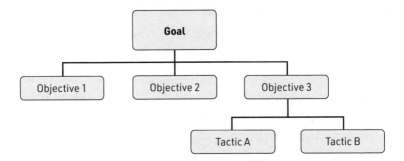

Figure 4.5 Hierarchy of goals, objectives, and tactics.

To further illustrate the hierarchy between goals, objectives, and tactics, consider a food refrigeration technology company that Dr. Evans advised. The primary goal of the company was market differentiation, expressed in the statement, "We will succeed by creating refrigerated vehicles with innovative features that our competitors cannot match and that allow us to charge a price premium to customers." Here are the objective and tactics supporting that goal:

- **Goal**: Market differentiation
- **Objective**: Be recognized by the industry as the leading innovator in the space of refrigerated food transportation technology
- **Tactic 1**: Launch new Bluetooth-enabled container that

transmits temperature data of the food from inside each of the boxes while in transit

- **Tactic 2**: Send out data collected from long-haul trips to influential retailer refrigerated food buyers inviting them to demo the technology

Figure 4.6 lays these elements out visually.

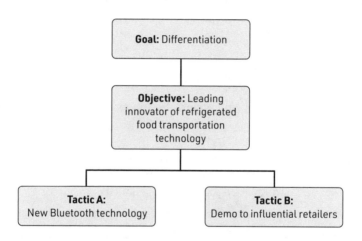

Figure 4.6. Illustrative example of the hierarchy of goals, objectives, and tactics.

WORDS OF CAUTION

Although we have included tactics in this chapter, they are not part of stage 4. This stage ends with goals and objectives, and we'll save the tactics for the next step in the process. We have only included tactics because, from our experience, many people operate at the lower level of tactics, and, when they are challenged to create goals and objectives, they often include a fair share of tactics. According to our strategy model, tactics start appearing as we cascade goals and objectives into departments and individuals in stage 5.

In developing strategy for a university, the team insisted that tactics were to be an integral part of the strategic decisions. Although Prof. Tim explained that tactics would be introduced as we cascade the goals and objectives into departments and individuals, the team rejected this explanation because it wasn't what they were used to. Prof. Tim allowed this inclusion as an exception. However, when it came to creating scorecards for departments and individuals, as explained in the next chapter, the process became overly complex because they were dealing with low-level operational details. They were forced to go back and review the strategic decisions and leave only goals and objectives. This can add time and expense to your entire strategy process.

Finally, one big mistake most organizations make is a lack of review of their goals and objectives by their stakeholders. This leads to people later working on tactics that do not align with the overall strategy. Therefore, make it a habit to review the goals and objectives regularly as a way of aligning tactical efforts to the desired strategy.

TAKING ACTION

WHY

The purpose of making strategic decisions is to choose a few critical priorities that will generate the greatest success. Once these have been determined, it is important for all stakeholders who will influence the development or achievement of goals, objectives, or tactics to understand the strategic themes, as well as why they were chosen and how they will guide the organization to superior performance.

WHAT

It is valuable for relevant stakeholders to understand the cascading nature of strategic themes toward goals, which then cascade into objectives and tactics. Stakeholders should develop a clear understanding of the difference among goals (what), objectives (how), and tactics (activities). Continually connecting all these decisions back to the strategic themes will ensure that the organization doesn't get sidetracked in the next two stages of strategy: planning and execution.

WHEN

Strategic decisions (themes, goals, and objectives) should be communicated generally as soon as they have been established. They should then be distributed quickly to the departments, teams, and individuals who will be responsible for creating and implementing the execution plan.

WHO

The broader these strategic decisions are communicated with stakeholders, the greater the chances of success. The only caveat at this point in the strategy process is to deliberate whether overcommunicating is counterproductive, such as revealing too much to potential competitors or other potential adversaries (suppliers, regulators, and others).

HOW

Well-designed documents that capture the substance and essence of strategic themes will be a great point of reference through the remaining stages of creating a strategy for results. In addition, these documents should be explained and emphasized through a variety of communication media that will provide clarity and enthusiasm going forward.

KEY TAKEAWAYS

TOOLS

- ABCD prioritization framework
- Resource–return grid
- The SAFe-A method

PEOPLE

- A combination of senior leaders focused on strategic themes and goals, with other leaders focused on objectives, both strategic and tactical
- People with decision-making, planning, and organizing skills

RESULTS

- Strategic themes
- Goals
- Objectives

STAGE 5

— ▲ —

STRATEGIC PLANNING
FOR EXECUTION

xecution is not a well-understood concept. Many people imagine
that it is the tactical side of business. But Bossidy and Charan
refute this and argue that although tactics are central to execution, execution is not tactics. They clarify,

> execution is a systematic process of rigorously discuss-
> ing hows and whats, questioning, tenaciously following
> through, and ensuring accountability. It includes making
> assumptions about the business environment, assessing
> the organization's capabilities, linking strategy to oper-
> ations and the people who are going to implement the
> strategy, synchronizing those people and their various dis-
> ciplines, and linking rewards to outcomes.[1]

Execution involves cascading the strategy developed in stage 4
into lower-level operational plans and assigning them to individuals
and teams with the requisite capabilities for successful implementation. It also includes implementing the operational plans to realize

results, monitor and evaluate the implementation, and reward people and teams that meet their targets. The latter is the subject of our sixth stage. Figure 5.1 shows the key processes of stage 5.

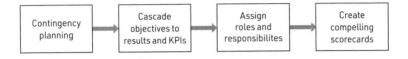

Figure 5.1. Stage 5 processes.

CONTINGENCY PLANNING

Contingency planning is based on the analysis of potential scenarios if significant changes in the way the organization runs its business take place (e.g., a particular change triggers a relevant planning question). The following is a list of possible contingency planning scenarios and questions to ask:

- If a major competitor withdraws from particular markets as intelligence reports indicate, what actions should our firm take?
- If our sales objectives are not reached, what actions should our firm take to avoid profit losses?
- If demand for our new product exceeds plans, what actions should our firm take to meet the higher demand?
- If certain disasters occur, what actions should our firm take?
- If a new technological advancement makes our new product obsolete sooner than expected, what actions should our firm take?

The organization must evaluate its capabilities as part of generating options, and these contingencies must be evaluated frequently to ensure readiness in the organization.

To create effective contingency plans, we must first identify both favorable and unfavorable events that could possibly derail the strategy or strategies. We often use the four contexts of utopian, doomsday, preferred, and probable to create divergent thinking.

For example, a university client was forced to assess face-to-face instruction at the onset of the COVID-19 pandemic. The utopian scenario would be that the pandemic is contained in the short term and the university continues on its student enrollment growth trajectory. The doomsday scenario would be that the pandemic would not be contained in the medium term and that neither face-to-face nor virtual lectures would be possible. The preferred scenario would be that the university switch to a combination of in-person and remote teaching, a strategy that the university was contemplating. The probable scenario would be that the pandemic would not be contained in the medium term, making it impossible to have in-person teaching and leaving only the virtual option.

Next, we need to specify trigger points, such as national COVID-19 restrictions for in-person meetings. Then, we assess the impact of each contingent event and the counter impact of each contingency plan. For example, the university would assess the cost of changing the teaching infrastructure to allow students on campus in strict adherence to COVID-19 protocols. The university would also assess the cost of transitioning to virtual teaching, including training both faculty and students and acquiring video conferencing and collaboration platforms.

We will then determine the early warning signs for key contingent events, such as significant numbers of students and faculty on campus becoming infected, which would necessitate closure of the campus.

Finally, for contingent events with reliable early warning signs, we must develop advance action plans to take advantage of the available lead time. For instance, when it becomes necessary, the university must be ready to close the campus, remove students and faculty from campus, and be ready to switch to online learning.

The organization must specify which of the scenarios it will be adopting for detailed planning. With clarity on the trigger points to transition to a different scenario, after an evaluation—for example, during quarterly monitoring or annual evaluations—your organization can make this change when it deems it necessary.

KEY RESULTS AND KPIS

To plan for execution, the objectives developed in stage 4 can be cascaded into key results, key performance indicators (KPIs), key initiatives, and actions, as is shown in the framework in figure 5.2.

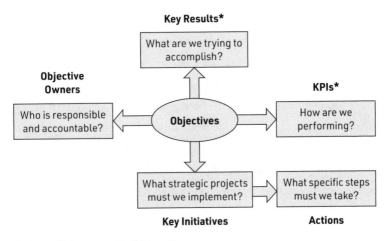

Figure 5.2. Cascading objectives.

Key results

Results-based management conceptualizes results as a progression of three types of results, referred to as a "results chain." Figure 5.3 shows a framework that we use to distinguish among the levels of results. The lowest level is outputs, followed by outcomes, with the highest level being impacts. Outputs are tangible practices, products, and services that are the consequence of completed activities. These, together with resources (to the left in figure 5.3), are detailed execution elements that are dealt with in stage 6. Impacts, on the other hand, are changes or effects on society that follow from achieved outcomes in the long term. Impacts are also subject to the influence of many other factors beyond strategy and often emerge beyond the typical medium-term planning horizons in most organizations. We propose that the long-term vision is the only strategy element that can be related to impact. Therefore, we focus on outcomes; these are our *key results*.

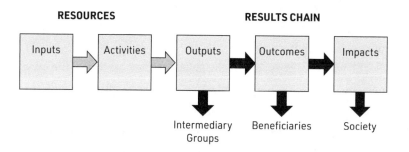

Figure 5.3. Results chain and its links to resources

Outcomes represent change in behavior, practice, or performance, on the part of the beneficiaries, that results from the delivery of outputs in the medium term. These outcomes are what a medium-term strategy is meant to achieve, and they form the basis for impact in the long term.

They are also subject to many other influences that may not be in the direct control of the strategy actors.

Improved employee engagement is an example of an outcome in a people theme. You will note that we used the word "improved" to indicate the direction in which we wish to change this outcome; this is because key results need to have a direction, a change toward something. We therefore use relevant "appropriate adjective" before the outcome to indicate the direction of the change in the outcome.

Key performance indicators

KPIs are used to indicate whether we are achieving the key results. They answer the questions, "How will we know success when we see it?" or "How will we know the desired changes have been realized?" They are used to set performance targets and assess whether we are making progress in monitoring and evaluating them. They tell us whether a change has occurred and whether any progress is being made toward our key results. They can be a critical source of information about whether our strategy is bearing fruit. Selecting the right indicator is vital to effective monitoring and evaluation.

There are two types of indicators: leading and lagging.[5] A financial indicator, such as revenue amount, for example, is a lagging indicator because it tells you about what has already happened. A people indicator, however, such as level of employee engagement, points to future performance and is therefore a leading indicator. This is because highly engaged employees are more likely to achieve higher productivity, which would lead to increased corporate performance. To build an accurate understanding of performance, it is important that we have a combination of these two types of indicators for a result.

---

5   A leading indicator looks toward future outcomes and events. A lagging indicator, on the other hand, looks back at whether the intended result was achieved.

Table 5.1 shows a canvas that we use to relate key results and KPIs to objectives and goals. As explained in stage 4, a goal will have a number of objectives. In our experience, you should not have more than five objectives for one goal; more than five normally indicates that there is more than one goal. If each objective is defined well, it should have one key result. In our experience, each result should have one or two KPIs. If you end up with two indicators of a result, it is best that one is a leading indicator and the other a lagging indicator. In the canvas, we have adopted a numbering structure that ensures that we can associate a KPI to a result, a result to an objective, and an objective to a goal. This makes tracking during execution much easier and lends itself to automation.

Table 5.1 shows a hypothetical example of the results and KPIs canvas for two themes for a hotel strategy.

Table 5.1 Key results and KPIs canvas example				
Themes	**Goals**	**Objectives**	**Key results**	**KPIs**
Theme 1: Customer	Goal 1: To become customer-centric	1. Develop and implement a customer retention strategy	Enhanced customer retention	Customer retention rate (%)
		2. Carry out regular customer surveys and implement recommendations		
		3. Implement a customer relationship management system		
		4. Upgrade the accommodation and dining infrastructure to attract high-income customers	Increased high-income clients	High-income clients (% of total clients)

Table 5.1 Key results and KPIs canvas example				
Themes	**Goals**	**Objectives**	**Key results**	**KPIs**
Theme 2: People	Goal 2: To enhance people performance	1. Review and implement a diversity strategy	Improved diversity in the organization	Degree of employee diversity (%)
		2. Review HR policy; implement a human resource management system	Increased efficiency of people processes	Reduced time to carry out annual performance appraisal (days)
		3. Develop and implement a talent development program	Enhanced organizational performance	Average performance appraisal rating (%)

ASSIGNING ROLES AND RESPONSIBILITIES

Strategy execution provides a wonderful opportunity to engage departments and motivated individuals in the creation of results. At the departmental or functional level, Prof. Tim often assigns corporate goals and objectives, as shown in table 5.2, for the example shown in table 5.1. That is, each department negotiates its contribution to each goal and its attendant objectives based on its specialization and capabilities. The completed canvas becomes critical in balancing workload among the departments as well as in resource allocation. The canvas is also used in assigning responsibility in the following corporate scorecard.

Themes	Goals	Objectives	M&S	F&B	HK	HR	Ops	IT
		Table 5.2. Canvas example for assigning goals and objectives to departments						
Theme 1: Customer	**Goal 1: To become customercentric**	Develop and implement a customer retention strategy	90%	0%	0%	0%	10%	0%
		Carry out regular customer surveys and implement recommendations	90%	0%	0%	0%	10%	0%
		Implement a customer relationship management system	50%	5%	5%	0%	0%	40%
		Upgrade the accommodation and dining infrastructure to attract high-income customers	0%	25%	30%	5%	30%	10%
Theme 2: People	Goal 2: To enhance people performance	Review and implement a diversity strategy	5%	5%	5%	75%	5%	5%
		Review HR policy; implement a human resource management system	3%	3%	3%	50%	3%	38%
		Develop and implement a talent development program	5%	5%	5%	75%	5%	5%

Abbreviations: *F&B: food and beverages department; HK: housekeeping department; HR: human resources department; IT: information technology department; M&S: marketing and sales department; Ops: operations department.*

This exercise became the subject of a heated debate in one of the strategy assignments Prof. Tim undertook for a medium-size technology company. It soon became clear that there were fuzzy boundaries in the mandates of the various departments. We eventually managed to agree on shared responsibilities among the departments, but this argument created a new strategic option: to review the organizational structure.

At the individual level, it is critical that we assign roles and responsibilities to the individuals most capable of optimizing the relevant aspects of strategy. As a leader, you will need to take several factors into consideration in determining who should be responsible for what, including

- The talents and skills of individuals in the context of the jobs to be done

- The availability of individuals to fulfill the various roles of execution (i.e., their bandwidth and the relevance of the strategy work to their overall responsibilities in the organization)

- The implications of assignments in relationship to the roles that individuals play as part of teams inside the organization, including the positional roles each individual plays, and whether they will serve to amplify or diminish effectiveness in the optimization of strategy

- The informal influence individuals yield throughout the organization and the implications of this influence in amplifying or diminishing the optimization of your strategy[2]

- The career and professional development opportunities for individuals inherent in the assignment of roles and responsibilities

In assigning roles and responsibilities, we need to balance the complexity of organizational needs with the specialization and capabilities of departments, as well as with the aspirations of individuals, as shown in the example in table 5.3.

CREATING COMPELLING SCORECARDS

There are three key principles that Ron employs in optimizing strategy. They are clarity, focus, and the measurement of progress or performance. All three principles are captured through the creation of compelling scorecards for the organization, for various teams, and ultimately, for individuals.

Table 5.3 shows a canvas Prof. Tim has successfully used for a corporate scorecard, with an example continued from tables 5.1 and 5.2. The objectives, key results, and KPIs, shown in italics, are those captured in the canvas in table 5.1. The baseline is the value of a specific indicator in the year before the beginning of the plan period, and the target is the value of the indicator in plan years (in this example, a three-year planning horizon). The next three columns show the target for each KPI and the year when that target would be achieved. For each KPI and target, we assign a specific officer in the responsibility column, as shown in the last column of table 5.3. In situations where we have more than one officer, as in the case of the high-income clients' KPI, the first-mentioned officer in this column takes primary responsibility. The others play a supporting role.

					Target & Timing			
Themes & Goals	**Objectives**	**Key Results**	**KPIs**	**Base-line**	**Y1**	**Y2**	**Y3**	**Respon-sibility**
Theme 1: Customer **Goal 1:** **To become customer-centric**	*Develop and imple-ment a customer retention strategy* *Carry out regular customer surveys and implement recommendations* *Implement a customer relation-ship management system*	*Enhanced customer retention*	*Customer retention rate (%)*	65	70	75	80	M&S Manager
	Upgrade the accom-modation and dining infrastructure to attract high-income customers	*Increased high-income clients*	*High-income clients (% of total clients)*	5	10	15	25	Ops Manager, HK Man-ager, F&B Manager
Theme 2: People **Goal 2:** **To enhance people perfor-mance**	*Review and imple-ment a diversity strategy*	*Improved diversity in the organi-zation*	*Degree of employee diversity (%)*	10	15	20	25	HR Manager
	Review HR policy; implement a human resource manage-ment system	*Increased efficiency of people processes*	*Reduced time to carry out annual perfor-mance appraisal (days)*	10	5	2	2	HR Manager, IT Manager
	Develop and implement a talent development program	*Enhanced organiza-tional per-formance*	*Average perfor-mance appraisal rating (%)*	63	65	70	75	HR Manager

Table 5.3: An Example of a corporate scorecard

Table 5.3 can be cascaded to the departments or functions and even further to teams or individuals responsible for specific KPIs and targets. As we carry out this cascading, we begin to show more implementation details and restrict the time to the first year of the strategy execution. For example, at the departmental level, we introduce specific initiatives, outputs, and targets that the department will take responsibility for in the corporate key results and targets to which they have capacity to contribute.

Examples of a departmental and an individual scorecard that we use are shown in tables 5.4 and 5.5, respectively. For table 5.4, we give an example of the marketing and sales department for the hypothetical case we have been using thus far. For table 5.5, we chose one departmental initiative in theme 1 for the head of sales. To ensure alignment, the first four columns in the departmental scorecard (shown in italics) are those from the corporate scorecard in table 5.3. Similarly, the first four columns in the employee scorecard (shown in italics) are from the departmental scorecard in table 5.4.

It is normal practice to restrict the timing in both the departmental and employee scorecards to the first year of execution of the strategy, and we recommend doing so. Some organizations find additional benefit in creating the scorecards for 90- or 100-day plans.

Themes & Goals	Objectives	Key Results	KPIs	M&S Initiatives	Required Resources	Output KPIs/ Targets	Timing	Respon-sibility
Theme 1: Customer **Goal 1: To become customer-centric**	*Develop and implement a customer retention strategy*			Carry out a survey on existing customers	USD 1,000	Analyzed survey results	Feb 2022	Head of Sales
	Carry out regular customer surveys and implement recommen-dations	*Enhanced customer retention*	*Customer retention rate (%)*	Develop a customer retention strategy	Internal workshop	Approved strategy	Feb 2022	Head of Market-ing
				Implement customer retention strategy	USD 5,000	70% customers retained	Dec 2022	Head of Market-ing
	Implement a customer relationship manage-ment (CRM) system			Implement a CRM system	USD 30,000	Signed UATs for all modules	Jun 2022	Head of Market-ing, IT Manager
	Upgrade the accom-modation and dining infrastruc-ture to attract high-income customers	*Increased high-income clients*	*High-income clients (% of total clients)*	N/A	N/A	N/A	N/A	N/A

Table 5.4: An example of a departmental scorecard

Table 5.4: An example of a departmental scorecard								
Themes & Goals	Objectives	Key Results	KPIs	M&S Initiatives	Required Resources	Output KPIs/ Targets	Timing	Respon- sibility
Theme 2: People **Goal 2: To enhance people perfor- mance**	Review and implement a diversity strategy	Improved diversity in the organiza- tion	Degree of employee diversity (%)	Review diversity in M&S Dept	None	Level of diversity	Mar 2022	M&S Man- ager, HR Manager
				Improve diversity in M&S Dept	Recruit new employees	5% improve- ment in Dept diversity	Dec 2022	M&S Manager
	Review HR policy Implement a human resource manage- ment system	Increased efficiency of people processes	Reduced time to carry out annual perfor- mance appraisal (days)	N/A	N/A	N/A	N/A	N/A
	Develop and implement a talent devel- opment program	Enhanced organiza- tional per- formance	Average perfor- mance appraisal rating (%)	N/A	N/A	N/A	N/A	N/A

Key:	Dept: Department	N/A: Not applicable

It is to be noted that some KPIs will not be relevant to some departments. This is why we have a few "Not applicable" entries on the table. In order to make the departmental scorecards short and concise, it is nor- mal practice to exclude those objectives, key results, and KPIs that are not relevant.

Table 5.5: An example of an employee scorecard for the Head of Sales							
Objectives	Key Results	KPIs	M&S Initiatives	Employee Activities	Required Resources	Start Date	End Date
Goal 1: To become customercentric							
Develop and implement a customer retention strategy	*Enhanced customer retention*	*Customer retention rate (%)*	*Carry out a survey on existing customers*	Develop a survey tool	Data on existing customers	Jan 2022	Jan 2022
				Pilot the survey tool		Jan 2022	Jan 2022
				Collect data	Online tools	Jan 2022	Feb 2022
				Analyze data		Feb 2022	Feb 2022
Carry out regular customer surveys and implement recommenda-tions			*Develop a customer retention strategy*	*N/A*	*N/A*	*N/A*	*N/A*
Implement a customer relationship management (CRM) system			*Implement customer retention strategy*	*N/A*	*N/A*	*N/A*	*N/A*
			Implement a CRM system	*N/A*	*N/A*	*N/A*	*N/A*
Upgrade the accommodation and dining infrastructure to attract high-income customers	*Increased high-income clients*	*High-income clients (% of total clients)*	*N/A*	*N/A*	*N/A*	*N/A*	*N/A*

We have witnessed organizations that have mastered using effective scorecards for themselves. The balanced scorecard methodology popularized by Kaplan and Norton is a good example of a holistic approach to organizational performance that can provide clarity, focus, and measurement at the organizational level.[3] However, without creating relevant, clear scorecards at the team and individual levels, focus and the measurement of performance often suffer.

Ron has effectively used the Gantt chart, named after Henry Gantt, who developed the first iterations of this scorecard between 1910 and 1915, for team and individual scorecards. Components of a Gantt chart that help optimize strategy include: specific jobs or tasks to be completed, a timeline with milestones for completion, and individual assignments of these tasks to establish clear, unambiguous accountability.

When optimized fully, there is a clear and visible connection from the individual scorecard to the team scorecard to the organizational scorecard. Or, in reverse, the organizational scorecard brings clarity to strategic themes and goals, the departmental and team scorecards bring clarity to objectives and tactics, and the individual scorecards bring clarity to KPIs and tasks.

These scorecards should bring SMART (specific, measurable, achievable, relevant, and timebound) direction to the KPIs, results, objectives, goals, and strategic themes for clarity, focus, and measured performance.

Once the scorecards have been created, simple stoplight coding provides a highly motivating and clear measurement of performance. You can use green highlighting to indicate completion or a task that is on track within the timelines, yellow to represent progress with some slippage from the timelines, and red to indicate a task or goal in danger of not being completed on time.

MONITORING AND EVALUATION

Monitoring is the process of continually tracking the implementation of planned programs or initiatives to assess their progress and performance. Evaluation, on the other hand, is the determination of the extent to which established goals, objectives, and results have been successfully met. Monitoring and evaluation together provide regular and timely information in support of evidence-based decision-making that serves as a key driver toward the realization of an organization's goals, objectives, and results. The prepared information includes progress that has been made, challenges that have been encountered, and any emerging issues. This knowledge can also be used to promote a culture of learning and the application of lessons learned.

To monitor and evaluate performance, every employee and team is expected to have the capacity to conduct a self-assessment and to report their performance within the agreed-upon scorecards discussed earlier. In our experience, the simplest framework to monitor performance is to add additional columns to the scorecards—namely, actual achievement, color-coded success (stoplight coding), and explanations for over- or underachievement. An example of a monitoring template for the marketing and sales department discussed earlier is shown in table 5.6. Monitoring can be at increments of weekly to monthly, quarterly, or, in some cases, semiannually, to optimize performance.

Table 5.6: Example of a departmental performance monitoring template								
Objectives	Key Results	KPIs	M&S Initiatives	Required Resources	Output KPIs/ Targets	Achievements		Explanations for over- or under- achievement
						Actual	RAG	
Goal 1: To become customer-centric								
Develop and implement a customer retention strategy			Carry out a survey on existing customers	USD 1,000	Analyzed survey results	100%		
Carry out regular customer surveys and implement recommen- dations	Enhanced customer retention	Customer retention rate (%)	Develop a customer retention strategy	Internal workshop	Approved strategy	100%		
			Implement customer retention strategy	USD 5,000	70% customers retained	60%		Strategy was not fully implemented
Implement a customer relationship manage- ment (CRM) system			Implement a CRM system	USD 30,000	Signed UATs for all modules	50%		There was resistance to change
Upgrade the accommo- dation and dining infra- structure to attract high- income customers	Increased high- income clients	High-income clients (% of total clients)	N/A	N/A	N/A	N/A	N/A	

Table 5.6: Example of a departmental performance monitoring template								
Objectives	*Key Results*	*KPIs*	*M&S Initiatives*	*Required Resources*	*Output KPIs/ Targets*	**Achievements**		**Explanations for over- or under- achievement**
						Actual	**RAG**	
Goal 2: To enhance people performance								
Review and implement a diversity strategy	Improved diversity in the organi- zation	Degree of employee diversity (%)	Review diversity in M&S Dept	None	Level of diversity	100%		
			Improve diversity in M&S Dept	Recruit new employ- ees	5% improve- ment in Dept diversity	0%		There was no opportunity to recruit new employees
Review HR policy *Implement a human resource man- agement system*	Increased efficiency of people processes	Reduced time to carry out annual performance appraisal (days)	N/A	N/A	N/A	N/A	N/A	
Develop and implement a talent devel- opment program	Enhanced organiza- tional per- formance	Average performance appraisal rating (%)	N/A	N/A	N/A	N/A	N/A	

In the case of evaluation, the template will have an additional set of lessons learned. This provides an opportunity for the actors to interrogate the execution and results and find insights on how, what, and where to improve or change for the next planning cycle.

Monitoring should be done internally by individuals and departments. However, for evaluation, we have found it expedient to use an external expert to ensure that there is honest, objective, and skillful conversation in evaluation and lessons learned.

Performance scorecards, depending on the organization's performance management practices, and monitoring and evaluation systems flow up from the individual or team levels to the department and corporate levels. Ideally, monitoring should be continuous, but, in our experience, organization-wide quarterly reviews are the most popular. We also have experience with some organizations choosing to monitor and/or evaluate semiannually or even annually. The ideal, or optimal, rhythm for monitoring and evaluating is context dependent, so it is important to adopt timing that provides the greatest probability of successful execution of strategy for your company.

TAKING ACTION

WHY

Successful strategic execution planning is about setting the team up for success. As such, it is critical that all contributors have a clear vision of how each layer of the cascading plans contributes to successful execution of the strategy. Activities and initiatives are validated by the KPIs and targets, which are validated by the objectives, which are validated by the goals, which emanate from the strategic themes. The overriding purpose of a plan is to provide clarity, ongoing focus, and a meaningful measurement of performance.

WHAT

The strategic execution plan should cascade down from broad to specific, with each new layer gaining more specificity, all the way to the detailed activities, targets, and timelines of teams and individuals. This planning system should then report results and insights from specific (individuals, teams) to broad (departments, offices, organizations), because these results connect to the goals, objectives, and strategic themes.

WHEN

The cascading of strategic execution planning is normally completed over a 30- to 90-day cycle, depending on the size and complexity of the organization.

WHO

Everyone in the organization should be involved in the development and communication of the plan in proportion to their authority and responsibility in execution.

HOW

The strategic execution plan should be designed and managed for superior performance as defined by the outputs and for a more long-term impact. As such, the details, review, and adaptation of the plan should be easily understood, consistently visible, and no more bureaucratic than is necessary to ensure success.

KEY TAKEAWAYS

TOOLS

- Key results and KPIs canvas
- Canvas for a corporate scorecard
- A departmental or functional scorecard
- An employee scorecard
- A departmental performance monitoring template

PEOPLE

- Department managers, team leaders, and individuals play the major role in creating the execution plan.
- Planning, organizing, project management, problem-solving, and negotiation are all important skills in creating the execution plan.

RESULTS

- Corporate implementation plan and its cascades to departments and individuals

PART 3

OPTIMIZING STRATEGY

Skills for success: planning and organizing, problem-solving, self-management, personal accountability, goal achievement, resiliency, flexibility, persuasion, negotiation, conflict management, teamwork, employee development and coaching, customer focus

STAGE 6

— ● —

STRATEGIC EXECUTION

W e have a plan. It is strong and achievable, and now it is specific. It's time to get to work! There are several obstacles to overcome throughout the seven stages of strategy. When work has been completed in one stage, the shift to the next always requires a new set of activities, skills, and energy. New people are activated and empowered as one stage opens to another.

The overarching principle of successful strategy execution is much like getting everyone rowing in the same direction. One of our colleagues, Whit Mitchell, coached crew at the collegiate level. He often reminds us that it isn't enough to just get everyone rowing in the right direction; the key to success is getting everyone rowing in the right direction and in sync![1]

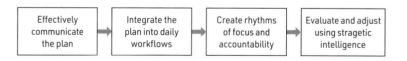

Figure 6.1. Stage 6 processes.

EFFECTIVELY COMMUNICATING THE PLAN

Getting an organization in sync around a strategy requires consistent, multifaceted communication that starts with a continuous connection back to the underlying drivers of strategy through purpose, core values, and vision. Through our experience, we have discovered that breakdowns in communication are a major cause of underperformance and frustration. To help organizations optimize communication, we have developed 10 facets of effective communication.[2]

Keep it simple

Although the overall plan may contain tremendous complexity and detail, the big picture description needs to be captured in a simple message easily understood by everyone. At the other end of the spectrum, each individual contribution must also be described as simply as possible.

Prof. Tim usually summarizes the strategy of an organization into a single schematic that's in the form of a strategy house, as shown in figure 6.2, along with a hypothetical example of a small to medium sized enterprise providing e-payments and other digital financial services. The imagery of a house communicates that developing and executing a strategy are similar to designing and building a home. The elements that support the strategy are the foundation of the organization.

As was argued in stage 1, the purpose and core values form the bigger part of the foundation. They are shown at the bottom of the house. The bigger part of the strategy is composed of the strategic themes and their corresponding goals. They're broken into two categories: pillars and enablers. Pillars are strategic themes that directly drive the results that the organization seeks to achieve. They tend to be strategic themes that directly affect customers and are related to the core business. Enablers, on the other hand, are strategic themes that support the pillars (e.g., financial resources) in realizing the goals. They're related to the support functions.

In figure 6.2, we show an example with two pillars and three enablers. For each strategic theme (pillar or enabler), we provide a goal. We also show the objectives, key results, and key performance indicators (KPIs) for each strategic theme. However, due to limitations of space, we have only shown the market's strategic theme. At the apex of the house, the vision that is being pursued in the planning horizon is provided. With this house, the strategy can be communicated in one graphic, and you can display it in prominent parts of the office.

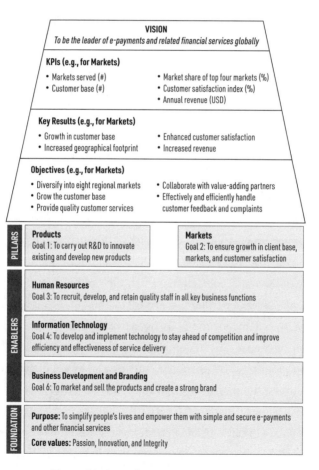

Figure 6.2. A simple communication strategy.

Keep it relevant

When people understand what's in it for them, they pay attention. Helping contributors see the big picture and how they make a difference helps the plan stick. For example, in the communication, individuals must be challenged to identify with and embody the purpose and core values in their day-to-day behaviors and activities. Similarly, the communication must illustrate how each person can contribute to the goals.

Repeat yourself

Continuously repeat yourself. The old advice to leaders is to communicate the plan until you are sick of hearing yourself, then communicate some more. Our advice is to keep communicating, but to continually find new ways to make the plan logical and inspiring. It is also important to regularly revisit the primary themes of the plan so your contributors don't begin to question your ongoing commitment, clarity, and focus on executing the strategic plan.

For example, the strategy will be communicated throughout the development process. During the launch of the strategy, Prof. Tim typically gets the board chair or CEO to communicate the foundation: purpose, vision, and core values. Then, each of the senior managers presents the pillar or enabler that is most relevant to their job. This presentation would include the goals, objectives, key results, and KPIs for the pillar or enabler. At the functional level, the head of each department communicates the corporate strategy as they get their people to focus on their functional contributions. This way, everyone will have heard the strategy from their leaders.

Ron once worked with an international organization to update their strategic plan for the first time in more than three years. There were a lot of people in the field who felt that creating a strategic plan was a silly exercise carried out for headquarters that wasn't relevant to their day-to-day operations. By developing detailed objectives and assignments under each goal and strategic theme, the planning's relevance became clear to everyone in the company. Next, they collaborated with their marketing department to publish the plan with details, icons representing each strategy theme, and pictures from various locations that made their field leaders better connect with the plan.

Use different media to communicate the strategy

"I sent everyone an email. Why don't they get it?" Great communicators continually think about the preferences of those they are communicating with and then adapt to a wide variety of modes of communication. Print, digital, visual, and audio are all varied modes of communication that affect people differently. Great communicators intentionally use all modes to maximize their impact and continually galvanize energy around the key strategic themes.

In Ron's example, the CEO also made a video that was distributed throughout the organization, expressing his commitment to the plan and the central role it would play with his leadership team through the coming year. This change in how they prepared and published the plan communicated that something was different from previous plans, which had had little impact on behaviors throughout the organization.

In several organizations that Prof. Tim has worked with, the strategy gets communicated through several media outlets. For example, an abbreviated version of the strategy (typically 5–10 pages), with lots of graphics, is sent to all employees and stakeholders; uploaded onto the organization's website and social media platforms; and embedded in audiovisual materials that can be sent as videos or act as screensavers, in branded materials with key messages from the strategy, and in an email as an attachment.

Adapt to various listening and reading styles

Some people just want the big picture; others need to dig deep into the details. Some will be focused on the *how*, whereas others will not be on board until they understand the *why*. Some audiences respond best to great storytelling and inspiration, and others want to see the inner workings of the strategy development. Some want all the background; others respond to bullet points. Some absorb and retain more of what they read, whereas others retain more through listening to the spoken word. By considering the most effective ways to help people connect with the plan, we set ourselves up for great impact and momentum.

The examples given under communicating the strategy using different media illustrate the different ways strategy can be communicated to suit different audiences and their preferences.

Be timely in responses and updates

Nothing causes the energy and focus on a strategic plan to fade quicker than a lack of attention from senior leadership. Taking an active role in responding to questions, concerns, and comments while also providing high-level updates on progress allows everyone to know that the strategic plan is the job to be done.

After the quarterly strategy execution reports are discussed by management and the board, it is normal practice to communicate—in great detail, to engage everyone—the status of execution of the strategy and the focus for the next quarter. The same is done after annual evaluations—that is, communicating what was achieved in the previous year and what plans there are for the next. In all this communication, it is important to highlight the key points in the board or management deliberations, what is coming next, and—most importantly—what is expected of the departments, teams, and individuals.

Use cascading messaging

There are some messages that should be delivered by senior management and others that are much more effectively communicated by others in the organization. Cascading communication starts at the top and works its way down, with greater detail and relevance, all the way to the individual contributor. In general, communication from the top represents what needs to be consistent throughout the company. As communication cascades throughout the organization, it should become more specific and directly relevant to those receiving the communication. Big picture issues and crisis management communication are almost always more effective coming from senior leadership.

For example, senior management should communicate purpose, vision, core values, goals, and key results. Middle management should get into lower-level details, including objectives, KPIs, key initiatives, tactics, or projects to be undertaken. At the operational level, communication involves activities and tasks, outputs, and delivery time frames.

Practice reciprocal conversations

The successful execution of strategy always requires communication in multiple directions. Think of a space mission and the constant communication that takes place throughout the entire team with transparency, timeliness, and mutual respect. Frontline workers often make observations that can have a profound impact on the successful execution of strategy. Cross-functional communication is required to optimize any strategic plan that has several moving parts. In total quality management[3] and constraint theory,[4] this is referred to as *optimization of the system*. The only way to optimize the entire strategy is to have continuous, reciprocal conversations.

For instance, while top management is focused on high-level strategic direction, line and operational management should simultaneously be thinking about what needs to be done at their level (e.g., at departmental and lower-unit levels). As senior management then communicates the strategic direction to lower-level units, these units also present what needs to be done and what can be executed at the operational interface with customers. The conversation that ensues improves both the strategic direction and the strategy at the operational level. Others have referred to this as adopting both a top-down and a bottom-up approach to strategy.

Remove distractions

Today, one of the greatest challenges to effective communication is peripheral noise, particularly in the increasingly digital space that most people work in. Practicing and advocating for present moment awareness in every communication means debunking the myth of multitasking and first demonstrating, then insisting, on active listening.

During strategic planning sessions with organizations, Prof. Tim likes to communicate rules that will govern his interactions with the teams. One rule is to be present and avoid disruptions from devices and work that people bring along everywhere they go. In most situations, the team will define a specific amount of money to be collected from anyone seen being distracted. A treasurer will be appointed to collect the fine, which will go into a drinks fund to be enjoyed at the end of the day or toward the workshop itself. In other situations, the fine might involve the offending person doing a traditional dance as a way to lighten the moment in the planning sessions. All possible distractions are allowed during breaks. Indeed, Prof. Tim would give the participants an extra half hour during lunch break to complete their distractions while he takes a power nap, an integral part of his day-to-day life.

Employ masterful feedback

Mastering feedback requires both receiving and providing constructive criticism that helps everyone in the organization know the current progress, next steps, and potential opportunities or challenges as the strategy continuously unfolds.[5]

It is normal for the strategic planning process to take several weeks, or even months, before a strategy emerges. Each of the stages described in this book represents an opportunity to communicate the outputs of that stage. This is why our strategy process model (figure 1.1) includes effective communication at every stage. For example, at the end of the foundation stage, communication of the purpose, a vision, and a long-term vision are created. Similarly, SLOC is communicated at the end of the strategic intelligence stage. This way, the strategy becomes fully owned by many individuals by the time the full-blown strategy emerges from the process. This ownership promises greater success during strategy execution.

INTEGRATING THE PLAN INTO DAILY WORKFLOWS

The work of executing a strategy must be integrated into your company's daily workflows so it is perceived as the job to be done rather than an extracurricular activity. Each employee should have clear vision as to how their work contributes directly or indirectly to the success of the plan. The more indirect the contribution, the more often the connection to the plan needs to be refreshed. You may need to review and update your employee, departmental, or functional scorecards to ensure they are clearly linked to the corporate strategy.

When individual contributors' work is broken down into specific tasks, activities, and behaviors that can be scheduled into days and weeks, the strategic plan comes alive. This is most effectively integrated on an individual level, with team and supervisory support. Setting aside time for detailed planning, organizing, and review helps establish and maintain prioritization of work on a daily and weekly basis. Organizations that don't do this end up with divided interests that result in weakened execution. The result is often leadership naivete about what it takes to achieve superior performance while also valuing the individuals who do that work. Proudly boasting how many extra hours our team members work and sacrifice in pursuit of the strategy should be viewed as a failure to effectively plan the daily workflows that honor people while achieving superior results.

CREATING RHYTHMS OF FOCUS AND ACCOUNTABILITY

The plan has a significantly greater chance for success when the organization creates various rhythms of focus and accountability that reach the individual contributor. These rhythms should be carefully considered based on the context and timelines for each contributor. In general, we recommend that performance reviews against the plan should take place according to the following schedule, purposely stated as bottom-up instead of top-down:

- Daily: Individual contributors with key colleagues
- Weekly: Key contributors with initiative champions

- Monthly: Initiative champions with senior leaders
- Quarterly: Senior leaders with the board of directors

These reviews provide the opportunity to celebrate progress and recognize those responsible, to identify areas where performance falls short of the plan, and to troubleshoot the obstacles. At monthly and quarterly reviews, there is opportunity to revisit the assumptions that went into creating the plan to determine whether circumstances require adjustments to optimize future performance.

The international organization Ron wrote about in stage 5 created an online tracking system (i.e., a dashboard) for every aspect of the strategy, which was visible to everyone in the organization. They also had monthly meetings with a senior leadership team to review their progress in executing the plan, with at least one senior leader responsible for monitoring and supporting the execution of each strategic theme. There was a larger review of the plan execution on a quarterly basis, with a broader group of leaders, including the board of directors. In these meetings, the leaders of each strategic theme reported on what had been accomplished over the past quarter, comparing their progress with the plan. They also reported new insights gained or changes in context, as well as what they would accomplish the next quarter. By making the execution of the strategic plan a consistent part of leadership team meetings, with new updates on a broad scale every quarter, the CEO and senior leaders finished the year with a great sense of accomplishment.

MAINTAINING FOCUS OVER TIME

In the agile framework, two regular practices have proven successful in moving strategy forward: the scrum and the sprint.[6] A scrum is a 10- to 15-minute stand-up meeting every morning in which everyone on the team briefly reports on what they accomplished the day before, what they are focused on accomplishing currently, and one problem they are working to solve in the future. These short meetings help the team members see how they fit into the larger work and often result in team members helping each other with problem-solving (which takes place outside of the scrum).

The sprint is usually a two-week plan of work to be done that creates a healthy sense of urgency and a rhythm of progress. Sprints are also conducted at the team level, giving a greater sense of camaraderie and accountability, much the same way a sports team learns to work together toward a common goal, even though each member of the team plays a different role.

Dr. Evans has used scrums and sprints with a number of clients to create and maintain clarity, transparency, accountability, and effective problem-solving amid great complexity and intense timelines.

There is also considerable room to explore new ways of sharpening clarity, focus, and accountability. How might you visualize your progress more dramatically? Some companies have large, visual representations of the progress being made toward strategy execution. These visual representations of the strategy help everyone in the organization see the progress being made, as well as their role in its success. What parts of strategic execution might be gamified, creating a healthy competition based on your goals and more frequent ways of feeding the organizational energy through recognition?

Ron worked with a team that had accepted an ambitious strategic goal that would have a lasting impact on the development of the company's future leaders. The magnitude of the goal provided a convenient excuse for compromise or falling short of the desired result, so Ron discussed with the CEO a special incentive for the team. The CEO agreed that if they hit all their deadlines and achieved the results as defined in the plan, everyone on the team would go on a weekend golfing trip with their significant others. However, if they failed, they would become the luggage haulers at the next annual conference for company employees. In doing this, everyone in the company would realize that they had failed to achieve their goal. In retrospect, the natural competitiveness in the company's culture created great energy for them to achieve more than what was expected.

Where can we create team-based opportunities for collaboration and celebration? Any time a strategic goal is shared by more than one department and there is clear definition of each person's, team's, and department's contributions, the shared interests will stimulate greater collaboration and celebration.

American football is a great example of this. There is only one goal that all members of a professional football team share: to win a Super Bowl game. The achievement of this single goal makes everyone involved in it part of history. Apart from this goal, there are multiple subteams, such as offensive linemen, receivers and running backs, quarterbacks, defensive backs, linebackers, and defensive linemen. Each group has different goals, different statistics to measure performance, different meeting rooms, different coaches, and plenty of opportunity for conflict or complaining. They often have friendly competitions among themselves. However, the one overarching goal of winning the big game forges the overall team into a connected unit. After a Super Bowl win, it's common to hear players say, "I love these guys" and "We did it together!"

Because most of strategic execution is undertaken by younger employees, the more you align with what holds their attention and builds their enthusiasm, the easier successful execution will become.

Ron worked with a client that refined their KPIs for the entire company (with more than 35 locations) down to one sheet. Every Monday morning, the senior leadership team met at 10 o'clock to review data from the previous week. This weekly review gave leaders an important view of how the business was responding to a number of external variables that could significantly impact their performance. It also gave them real-time insights into how each of their locations was adapting to the constantly changing environment.

We have worked with a number of clients who find it beneficial to monitor individual and team progress weekly, departmental and functional progress around strategic themes monthly, and overall organizational performance with senior management and their boards quarterly.

EVALUATING AND ADJUSTING YOUR USE OF STRATEGIC INTELLIGENCE

We have also worked with organizations that realized their plan was too modest or too demanding through regular reviews. Sometimes, new opportunities, challenges, or internal strengths and limitations emerge, creating enough change to justify adjustments to the plan.

We are aware of several businesses that had to review their strategy because of the challenges and opportunities presented by the COVID-19 pandemic. For example, an educational institution that Prof. Tim works with had to change the delivery of its programs and courses to online and create new revenue streams to cope with reduced tuition income. Another example is when the owner of a small business died unexpectedly, and no one knew what to do; they called Ron and his team to help them figure it out. While grieving the loss of their long-time owner, the team was also able to create clarity and structure for moving forward, which resulted in holding on to many high performers who were questioning their future job security.

Instead of the seven stages of strategy appearing linear and exclusive from one another, savvy organizations keep the functions and benefits of each stage in constant motion. Internal reviews of strengths and limitations should be ongoing and updated. External reviews of opportunities and challenges must be continually studied by internal think tanks, with new information informing everyone and resulting in minor (and sometimes major) adjustments and optimization of the strategic plan.

Instead of a new planning cycle starting every year or every three to five years, the strategy becomes an ongoing discussion about exploration of the seven stages, resulting in a dynamic, living organism that constantly adapts to and leverages changes through continuous strategic readiness.

Above all, the strategic execution plan is meant to serve the organization, rather than the organization serving the plan. A wise leader will recognize when it is appropriate to intensify focus and resources on a good strategy and when it is better to adjust because of new factors not present or known when the plan was created.

TAKING ACTION

WHY

Communication throughout the execution stage is critical to maintain focus, build momentum, and identify obstacles to success.

WHAT

There are two primary areas of communication that everyone in the organization should receive on a regular basis. The first is how the work closest to them is being accomplished and how their individual work or that of their team continues to contribute to or hinder success. The second is how the big picture is developing. Is it progressing on schedule with the goals and objectives related to the strategic themes? Are adjustments being made based on new circumstances? What kinds of problems have emerged? Who is making outstanding contributions to strategic execution? How is the strategy resonating with the organization's customers and other external stakeholders?

WHEN

Detailed work should be communicated with the relevant people on a daily or weekly basis. Progress on broader initiatives should be communicated monthly, at a minimum. And the progress toward successful achievement of goals, objectives, and key results should be communicated no less than quarterly.

WHO

Everyone throughout the organization should be informed of the part of the plan that is relevant to them and their work. In addition, the entire organization and external stakeholders, when relevant, should be updated on the overall execution of the plan.

HOW

Normally, monitoring and evaluating the execution of the plan should happen from the bottom up, with individuals and teams having weekly visibility meetings and senior management meeting no less than quarterly.

KEY TAKEAWAYS

TOOLS

- Framework for effective communication of the implementation plan
- Tools for integrating the implementation plans into daily operations
- Creating rhythm, focus, and accountability
- Evaluating and adjusting to optimize outcomes

PEOPLE

- Everyone in the organization has a part to play in execution.
- Skills for execution are broad, from planning and organizing to decision-making, problem-solving, self-management, negotiation, conflict management, teamwork, and more.

RESULTS

- Corporate and departmental operational and work plans
- Employee performance plans or contracts that integrate strategy execution into daily workflows and responsibilities
- Timely and accurate monitoring of plan execution

STRATEGIC EVALUATION AND LEARNING

> *Unless strategy evaluation is performed seriously and*
> *systematically and unless strategists are willing to act on*
> *the results, energy will be used up defending yesterday.*
> *No one will have the time, resources or will to work on*
> *exploiting today, let alone to work on making tomorrow.*
>
> **—PETER DRUCKER**

valuation is the process of determining the effectiveness of specific actions. Learning is the process of interrogating the process and the resulting actions to find insights on how, what, and where to improve or change the outcomes of the actions themselves or the process in which the outcomes were generated. In other words, learning is the process of improving actions and results through knowledge and understanding of the evaluation process. Evaluation and learning, which are complementary activities, should take place throughout the strategy management process.

Effective organizational learning is founded on asking numerous and contextual questions. Because the context in the organization is always changing, learning must be continuous and contextual. In answering questions about both content and context, and with proper engagement of data and stakeholders, insights are discovered and opportunities for improvement are clearly identified. Ultimately, the organization demonstrates learning by improving processes, activities, and results. And to maximize learning, we recommend using external facilitators who will challenge and encourage—and even cajole, when appropriate—much the same way an athletic coach pushes their athletes to new heights of performance.

THE IMPORTANCE OF STRATEGY EVALUATION AND LEARNING

The strategy evaluation and learning process has multiple benefits. It helps keep a check on the validity of your strategic choices. The ongoing process of evaluation and learning will, in fact, provide feedback on the continued relevance of the strategic choices made during the strategy creation phase. This is due to the efficacy of strategic evaluation to determine the effectiveness of the strategy. It helps assess whether decisions match the intended strategy requirements. It helps result in a successful culmination of the strategic management through its process of control, feedback, rewards, and review.

In the absence of an evaluation and learning process, managers would not know explicitly how to exercise such discretion. Evaluation and learning provide a considerable amount of information and experience to the organization that can be useful in new strategy planning and in maximizing the efficacy of the existing strategy.

Consequently, evaluation and learning should initiate managerial questions about expectations and assumptions; trigger a review of most strategy elements, including strategic themes, goals, objectives, purpose, vision, and values; stimulate creativity in generating alternative strategic options and formulating criteria for evaluation; and be performed on a continuing basis, rather than at the end of specified periods of time or just after problems occur.

EVALUATING STRATEGY RESILIENCE AND RELEVANCE

To effectively evaluate strategy development and execution, we have found the following to be useful: [1]

- Consistency: the strategy must not present mutually inconsistent goals and objectives.
- Adaptive: the strategy must represent a contextual response to the external environment and to the critical changes occurring within it.
- Advantage: the strategy must provide for the creation or maintenance of competitive advantage in a selected area of the activity.
- Feasibility: the strategy must neither overtax the available resources nor create unsolvable subproblems. It must also be developed and implemented within the physical, human, and financial resources of the enterprise.

EVALUATION AND LEARNING IN EACH STAGE

Evaluation and learning must be incorporated into each stage for preparation, creation, and optimization of the strategy. To effectively learn from each stage, it is helpful to use the build–measure–learn model,[2] shown in figure 7.1.

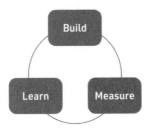

Figure 7.1. The build–measure–learn model.

This is how it works: Building takes place in step 1. In each stage, clearly define what needs to be accomplished and execute activities according to expectations. In step 2, measure. Measure the results of the activities in step 1. In step 3, learn. Analyze the results in step 2, then think about, gain insights from, and identify gaps (expected versus actual outcomes) in the results, and, finally, evaluate whether there are opportunities to improve the results. Step 1 has already been achieved as part of the strategy process. The focus in this section is to measure and learn (steps 2 and 3). We now review the key questions to ask in order to evaluate and learn in each of our seven stages of strategy.

STAGE 1

In stage 1 (establishing the foundation of strategy), evaluate the clarity of the purpose statement, the values of the organization and their alignment to the purpose, and the vision of the organization.

From a learning perspective, the key questions are

- What is it about the purpose of the organization that needs to be created or improved upon to ensure it reflects the founder's vision or the current thinking among stakeholders?

- How evident is the purpose of the organization to everyone who interacts with the organization?

- What can be improved to better align the purpose, values, and vision of the organization?

- Who must be involved to improve the level of alignment among the purpose, values, and vision of the organization?

- What is the feedback received on both the quality and method involved in formulating or updating the purpose, values, and vision? How can we improve the process of developing or updating the foundational elements of strategy?

- What level of resonance do we have between the organization's purpose, values, and vision, and the individual aspirations of leaders throughout the organization (and everyone is a leader!)?

STAGE 2

In stage 2 (building strategic intelligence), evaluate the clarity of the strategy, sources of data, the context of how the data is collected and analyzed, and the process of creating insights from such data.

From a learning perspective, the key questions are

- Are the processes, methods, and tools used in analyzing internal and external environments available, clear, easy to use, and accessible to all necessary stakeholders?

- Are the processes duplicable and precise enough to improve the reality and accuracy of the intelligence?

- How can we improve the processes of gathering strategic intelligence?

- Are the appropriate forums available to evaluate the data using different points of view and different facilitators to stimulate additional insights?

STAGE 3

In stage 3 (creative strategic thinking), evaluate the number, quality, and applicability of the strategic options.

From a learning perspective, the key questions are

- Are the tools and processes effective in generating as many ideas as possible, and how can they be improved? (Effective strategic options are best selected from a large number of ideas that have been generated from many sources and from different individuals.)
- How can we improve the way we engage stakeholders in the creative process?[3]

STAGE 4

In stage 4 (making strategic decisions), evaluate the results of the decision-making process.

From a learning perspective, the key questions are

- How can we improve the decision-making process regarding option selection?
- How can we enhance the quality of the options?
- What is the right forum to discuss the options?
- How accountable are we as an organization to the options we choose?
- What difficulties were experienced in differentiating the various goals, objectives, and tactics, and how can we address them?
- Are the goals and objectives both realistic and challenging?
- How likely is it that we will successfully achieve these goals and objectives?

STAGE 5

In stage 5 (strategic execution planning), evaluate reality or readiness to execute the strategy with the right accountability systems and metrics in place.

From a learning perspective, the key questions are

- How effective is our process of cascading goals and objectives to the operational level?
- What is the level of involvement of everyone in execution planning?
- How realistic are the departmental, team, and individual scorecards?
- Are the individual and team scorecards aligned to what motivates people?
- How can we improve the realism of the planning process so goals, objectives, and tactics are always on or close to the target? That is, do we have an 80 percent chance or better for success?

STAGE 6

In stage 6 (strategic execution), evaluate the relevancy and effectiveness of the execution of the strategic options.

From a learning perspective, the key questions are

- Is the data we are collecting in the specified intervals answering some key operational questions in a timely manner?
- How can we improve data collection and analysis?
- How can we improve monitoring and evaluation of performance?

- How can we accelerate what we are learning from the evaluation of performance?
- Ultimately, are we realizing the results expected of the strategy?

EFFECTIVE EVALUATION AND LEARNING SYSTEM

For the build–measure–learn model to work, the evaluation process must be simple, actionable, easy, and rewarding to execute. This means that

- You must involve only a minimum amount of viable information; too much or too little information creates confusion and is therefore ineffective.

- You should capture and monitor only activities and results that are relevant to your strategy's execution.

- Your activities must be specific and must relate to the objectives.

- The data of the activities must be timely so that corrective actions can be taken quickly.

- Your activities should provide an honest account of what is happening and must also be contextual.

- You must create processes that are engaging and sustainable so they can be adopted (similar to scrum and other agile methods).

- You must be able to easily identify exceptions (nitpicking does not result in effective evaluation). Focus on and emphasize the 80:20 principle, in which 20 percent of the activities result in 80 percent of the achievements.

- The activities, data analysis, and decision-making processes should foster mutual understanding, trust, and common use.
- The reward of meeting or exceeding standards should be emphasized so your managers are motivated to perform. A good rule of thumb is a recognition–criticism ratio of 3-to-1.
- You must avoid unnecessary emphasis on penalties, because they tend to pressurize the managers to rely on efficiency rather than effectiveness, as well as hinder transparency.

In addition to making the process simple, the organization must be willing to spend time thinking of the different contexts and data. To accomplish this, create forums and form teams that will examine the data. Encourage everyone involved to think deeply, widely, and boldly to uncover insights for the present and create better and smarter steps going forward. Learning is a thinking skill. This means that, as an organization, you must learn how to think and how to think well.

George Bernard Shaw wrote, "Two percent of the people think; three percent of the people think they think; and ninety-five percent of the people would rather die than think." Of course, Mr. Shaw was a writer and philosopher, not a scientist. As such, we interpret his statement as an admonition to keep improving our thinking skills instead of making the judgment that 98 percent of people are ignorant.

There are many barriers to overcome to effectively evaluate and learn from your strategy. These barriers include, but are not limited to, a lack of processes or structure, including the lack of appropriate forums for discussions and improvements; difficulties in measurements; resistance to evaluation; short termism, referring to leaders who do not stay in their roles long enough to experience the consequences of their strategic decisions; reliance on efficiency (doing things right) rather than on effectiveness (doing the right things); and gaps in leadership.

When management is committed to good-to-great strategy, most of these barriers can be overcome through the development of appropriate organizational structures and culture. We have worked with a number of clients who effectively review, evaluate, and learn from their results in a bottom-up flow, culminating in quarterly reviews that report and discuss what they are learning to their board of directors. More often than not, this practice of continuous evaluation and learning has resulted in more success, recognition, and endorsement from those in positions of governance.

CORRECTIVE ACTIONS

To demonstrate learning, you must act based on the insights gained during the evaluation and learning process. Although such action will vary depending on the strategy context, here are some examples of potential actions:[4]

- Alter the organization structure.
- Add or replace one or more key individuals.
- Divest a program or department.
- Alter the organization vision or mission.
- Revise objectives, key initiatives, outcomes, or KPIs.
- Devise new policies.
- Implement new performance incentives.
- Raise new or additional capital.
- Allocate resources differently.
- Outsource—or rein in—business functions.

TAKING ACTION

WHY

Communicating strategy evaluation and learning throughout the organization makes everyone smarter and helps maintain or build momentum toward the successful execution of strategy.

WHAT

Evaluation and learning should become a natural habit throughout the organization. Creating, improving, and expanding questions that are relevant, timely, and even provocative will help optimize strategy execution beyond the original possibilities.

WHEN

When evaluation and learning are habitually practiced throughout the organization, the process is continuous throughout each of the stages of strategy.

WHO

Everyone should believe they have the responsibility to evaluate and learn. Senior leaders carry the greatest responsibility to ensure this is encouraged and rewarded as part of the organizational culture.

HOW

Using and adding to the questions listed in each stage of strategy will help create an upward spiral of continuous learning and improvement.

Ask questions that are most likely to create the greatest learning opportunities, with the objective of optimizing your strategy always in mind.

KEY TAKEAWAYS

TOOLS

- A checklist for strategy evaluation
- The build–measure–learn model
- Key strategic learning questions for each stage

PEOPLE

- Everyone in the organization should participate in bottom-up forums.
- Valuable skills include continuous learning, personal accountability, flexibility, resiliency, problem-solving, teamwork, and others.

RESULTS

- Realized results
- Lessons from strategy development and execution

STRATEGY FOR RESULTS

When preparing for, creating, and optimizing strategy, we often ask the question, "What does *good* look like?" We offer the following three criteria in an effort to make the complex simple:

1. Good strategy must be shared.
2. Good strategy must be executable.
3. Good strategy must be measurable.

If you have made it this far, you have seen a multitude of concepts, processes, and tools. It is clear that the successful creation and optimization of a strategy requires rigor, tenacity, and adherence to a considerable amount of discipline. The results of all this work must justify the efforts—and we think it does. Strategy, well-conceived and executed, is a tremendous differentiator that provides any organization continuous opportunities for growth, insights, and competitive advantage.

What is wonderful about this opportunity is that it is not limited by resources; the only true limitations will be those you allow through a lack of commitment to ongoing clarity, focus, and measurement of progress. It seems appropriate to summarize with a reminder that mastering strategy is a never-ending journey to greater clarity, focus, and achievement.

AFTERWORD

BY JERRY SU,
managing director, Associated British Foods, Greater China

Strategy has become a regular part of the conversation in a lot of leadership meetings. People or managers often use it in a very shallow way. There are many books that explore strategy from different perspectives, but very few treat strategies as an eco-system that should include continuous reviewing, evaluating, and learning to optimize the strategy itself and to optimize results.

In my experience as an executive, there are a lot of common misperceptions and practices in the real world of business. We tend to use strategy as the core of executive leadership and think of it as either good strategy or bad strategy. We have systematized annual budget planning and forecasting, but we often miss the opportunities for regular review, evaluation, and learning across the strategy continuum.

Many have written that strategy is about making choices, but they often neglect to create enough strategic options that will give their organizations better choices in creating strategy that works. Managers often behave as if once they have developed a good strategy, great results will come naturally. They either neglect or are ignorant to the fact that for successful strategy execution they will need to engage in continuous communication, ongoing goals, and objectives that will connect strategy to the functional, individual KPI (key performance indicators), and employee engagement that are crucial to getting the best results.

This book provides a holistic process—tools to prepare for strategy, developing a large number of strategic options, focusing on the critical few strategy themes, and then the disciplines of strategy execution and learning.

In this VUCA world, with a faster speed of change, we need better knowledge about strategy development implementation. We need practical ways to realize and optimize our strategy for results. As a leader in this very dynamic environment in China, I have to empower every manager and individual to do their best. I need to ensure everyone wants to contribute because of a clear and meaningful purpose that is worth their maximum efforts. *Optimizing Strategy for Results* will guide leaders in developing strategy with clear company purpose, values, and vision that will inspire every individual in the organization. One of the most valuable benefits of this book is the insight it provides to bring the whole team together to drive results by recognizing each individual's role in creating success. This is a book about more than strategy!

I was particularly impacted by a statement toward the end: "Mastering strategy is a never-ending journey to greater clarity, focus, and achievement." I would like to add that this also helps our organizations have stronger alignment, stronger team members, and more inspired individuals through the evaluation and learning process.

Ron has been a good friend for many years, and he has been a coach who helped me turn around the business I lead today. Our relationship began when I assumed my leadership role for China in 2009. I am so happy to see him expand his influences to help more corporations through this book which is one of the best business books I have ever read.

BY JOSE FRANCISCO ORTIZ COLLADO,
former executive at Zoetis Animal Health (and Pfizer Animal Health)

Optimizing Strategy for Results and the model of the 7 stages in the strategic process that the authors present us is highly structured, systemic, and pragmatic and will help readers achieve precisely what they promise: results. How many times have we seen companies with elaborate strategic plans that look wonderful on paper and are no more than a good elaborate document without real achievements?

The concepts that the authors share with us definitely help establish the foundations of a strategic plan, guiding readers in their search for vision, aspiration, and—why not say it—the dream of where executives would like to take their companies. That is where the journey in developing a plan really begins, which should be supported by all those indicators, plus market and environment information that allow us to provide guidance even with the uncertainty we operate with today.

VUCA makes sense today more than ever, in front of the volatility, uncertainty, complexity, and ambiguity in which companies operate. From my own experience in creating and implementing strategy in undeveloped regions, I have seen the impact of disruptions more intensely than most. It is for this reason that the ten-year strategic plans that were developed previously have no reason to exist. They became documents that consumed a lot of effort and energy. In the end, those who created them rarely saw the work finished. In an environment governed by VUCA, it is more feasible to operate in a shorter scenario, such as 5 years, where we are not only exposed to change as a constant but also to the ever-increasing speed of this change.

The authors share from their own experiences how to create strategic thinking within organizations by engaging the greatest number and diversity of influencers from analysis to final plan, who, led by the organizational vision, are involved in creating the future of the company.

Even more important, the plan becomes a part of their own aspirations and commitments. It is not a question of Thinkers vs Doers as sometimes happens, nor should correct strategic planning follow a single direction. When strategy is created and optimized as explained in this book, the resulting inclusive and highly engaged individuals involved in preparing or creating and optimizing the strategy bring the fulfillment to the vision.

One of the most important points of the model presented by the authors has to do with decision-making. Personally, I have always believed that strategic planning should not only be supported by what we said we were going to do, but also by what we said we were *not* going to do. Based on these decisions, it is important to maintain consistency and what I call "strategic discipline" in the midst of competing interests.

Once the plan is developed, as the authors well point out, we must shift into a highly focused commitment to strategy execution. I believe it is not only a matter of starting to implement, but also to continually communicate and generate the ongoing motivation of the team so that the plan can be seen as aggressive but achievable, and then to cascade these concepts throughout the organization so that everyone can develop what I refer to as the General Manager Mindset.

When moving into Plan Execution stage, other critical factors for its success include ongoing inspiration, conviction, influence, and leadership by example. This energy and focus must be expressed by both the senior leader and the executive team of the organization. This creates a "make things happen" mindset within the organization. It cannot be emphasized too much how critical this is to optimize the strategy.

And so, we reach the last stage of the model, the evaluation and learning. This is where the concept of operationalizing the strategy becomes important by including the plan as part of our daily activities with periodic evaluations of progress through the analysis of indicators that allow us to celebrate the achievement of our objectives or to correct any deviations that may arise.

From my point of view, *Optimizing Strategy for Results* helps to lead, manage, and establish a continuous *process*, which will consequently ensure that the results are achieved. Without a doubt, you have in your hands a book that represents an excellent guide to get results.

ACKNOWLEDGMENTS

PROF. TIM

I would like to thank Professor Ndeti Ndati, director of the School of Journalism and Mass Communication at the University of Nairobi, for his meticulous editing of the initial draft of this book. I am also most indebted to Dr. Julius Kipng'etich, group CEO of Jubilee Insurance, and Dr. Fred Ogola, senior faculty at Strathmore Business School, at Strathmore University, for their candid perspectives of and suggestions to the first draft. There are many friends who were happy to endorse the book, including Dr. James Mwangi, group CEO of Equity Group; Dr. Julius Kipng'etich, group CEO of Jubilee Insurance; Dr. Vincent Ogutu, vice-chancellor designate at Strathmore University; and Dr. Charles Borura, chief manager of operations at the Kenya Revenue Authority, to whom I am most grateful. Finally, I cannot forget to appreciate in a special way my wife, Dr. Rosa Mwololo, and our three children, for their love and encouragement during the entire book project.

RON

It is difficult to find the words to express my gratitude for the collaboration that has taken place among Prof. Tim, Dr. Evans, and myself. We started talking about a book on strategy over two years ago, then had a serious discussion about collaborating in January 2020. We shared the same interests of helping organizations develop new skills and passion for strategy. We shared many values with each other, chief among them being respect for one another. Working together, we were able to discover, once again, the power of true collaboration. Each one of us contributed something unique to this book. It can be said, without hesitation, that none of us could have created this book without the contributions, insights, and encouragement of one another. Most of all, I'm grateful for the time I was able to spend (on Zoom) with these two amazing human beings.

The folks at Greenleaf Book Group have been wonderful to work with throughout the entire process. Nathan True did what all great developmental editors do—write lots and lots of notes, questions, and suggestions. Thank you, Nathan, for strengthening the manuscript in many different ways! Christine Florie added rigor as our copyeditor. Like other copyeditors, I love her commitment to strong writing and accurate citations. And thanks also goes to Dylan Julian, who added "polish" to the final result as our proof editor. Special thanks goes to Justin Branch, Lindsay Bohls, Lindsey Clark, Kimberly Lance, Chelsea Richards, and Kristine Pyre-Ferry, all part of our team at Greenleaf Book Group and, for this book, our liaisons with the Inc Original Imprint.

As Prof. Tim has written, we are grateful for the friends who agreed to review an early draft and who gave us valuable feedback. From my group of friends, this includes Rick Stott, CEO of Superior Farms; Dr. Tom Sechrest, director of the Mathematics and Statistics Learning Center and the Doctorate of Education of Leadership and Higher Education Program at St. Edward's University; William J. Russell, dean of the College of Business at Northwest Nazarene University; Tyler Andrew, CEO of the Better Business Bureau Great West and Pacific; Rob Fricker, business and leadership growth specialist at Simply

Superior Success; Dr. Lisa Aldisert, CEO of Pharos Consulting; and Dr. Francis Eberle, senior advisor at Price Associates. I am also grateful for the endorsements of our reviewers, plus those who see fit to post reviews online or send us feedback post publication.

Our clients also deserve our gratitude. They have given us the laboratories to test new ideas, discover new processes, and solve common problems around the preparation, creation, and optimization of strategy. And for those who read this book and share it with others, please accept our gratitude in advance.

Finally, so much of who I have become has been shaped by my family. My wife, Pam, has given me wide space to pursue my eclectic interests for almost 50 years; our six children and their spouses have been a continual source of learning and purpose; and our 10 grandchildren (at the time of this publication) remind me that our greatest privilege is to invest in others.

DR. EVANS

This project would never have been possible without the contributions of my coauthors, Prof. Tim and Ron. The content creation sessions and weekly meetings were energizing and insightful; I appreciate the collaboration and accountability. I am grateful for my family for their support throughout this project—forever grateful for them.

ENDNOTES

INTRODUCTION

1. "Leadership Skills & Strategies," VUCA-WORLD, accessed March 24, 2020, https://www.vuca-world.org/.

2. Nassim Talib, *Antifragile: Things That Gain from Disorder* (New York: Random House, 2012), 3.

3. Jim Collins and Morten T. Hansen, *Great by Choice* (New York: Harper Business, 2011).

4. Richard Rumelt, *Good Strategy Bad Strategy: The Difference and Why It Matters* (New York: Crown Business, 2011), page 5.

5. Hugh G. Courtney, Jane Kirkland, and S. Patrick Viguerie, "Strategy under uncertainty," McKinsey & Company, June 1, 2000, https://www.mckinsey.com/business-functions/strategy-and-corporate-finance/our-insights/strategy-under-uncertainty.

6. Michael Porter, *Competitive Strategy: Techniques for Analyzing Industries and Competitors* (New York: Free Press, 1998).

7. Henry Mintzberg, *The Rise and Fall of Strategic Planning* (New York: Free Press, 2013).

8. Ron Price and Stacy Ennis, *Growing Influence: A Story of How to Lead with Character, Expertise, and Impact* (Austin, TX: Greenleaf Book Group, 2018).

9. Mark W. Johnson and Josh Suskewicz, *Lead from the Future: How to Turn Visionary Thinking into Breakthrough Growth* (Cambridge, MA: Harvard

Review Press, 2020); Richard Pascale, Mark Milleman, and Linda Gioja, *Surfing the Edge of Chaos: The Laws of Nature and the New Laws of Business* (New York: Penguin Random House, 2001).

10. Ron Price and Randy Lisk, *The Complete Leader: Everything You Need to Become a High-Performing Leader* (Eagle, ID: Aloha Publishing, 2014).

STAGE 1

1. Verne Harnish and the Team at Gazelles, *Scaling Up: How a Few Companies Make It . . . and Why the Rest Don't* (Ashburn, VA: Gazelles Inc., 2014).

2. Peter Drucker, *Management: Tasks, Responsibilities, Practices* (New York: Harper & Row, 1973).

3. Simon Sinek, *Start with Why: How Great Leaders Inspire Everyone to Take Action* (London: Penguin Random House, 2009).

4. Verne Harnish and the Team at Gazelles, *Scaling Up: How a Few Companies Make It . . . and Why the Rest Don't* (Ashburn, VA: Gazelles Inc., 2014), 97.

5. Verne Harnish and the Team at Gazelles, *Scaling Up: How a Few Companies Make It . . . and Why the Rest Don't* (Ashburn, VA: Gazelles Inc., 2014).

6. Jim Collins and Jerry Porras, *Built to Last: Successful Habits of Visionary Companies* (New York: Harper Business, 2004).

7. Peter H. Diamandis and Steven Kotler, *The Future Is Faster Than You Think* (New York: Simon & Schuster, 2020). Audible version with coauthor conversations included.

8. There are several books that can help identify future trends. Some of our favorites include *The Anticipatory Organization* by Daniel Burrus, *Turning the Future into Revenue* by Glenn Hiemstra, and *The Next 100 Years* by George Friedman.

9. Daniel Burrus, *The Anticipatory Organization: Turn Disruption and Change into Opportunity and Advantage* (Austin, TX: Greenleaf Book Group, 2017).

STAGE 2

1. J. D. Mayer and P. Salovey, "What is emotional intelligence?," in *Emotional Development and Emotional Intelligence: Educational Implications*, eds. P. Salovey and D. J. Sluyter (New York: Basic Books, 1997), 3–31.

2. D. Goleman, *Working with Emotional Intelligence* (New York: Bantam Books, 1998); D. Goleman, *Emotional Intelligence: Why It Can Matter More Than IQ*, Revised Edition (London: Bantam, 2006), 281; D. Goleman, "What makes a leader?," *Harvard Business Review*, November–December 1998.

3. C. S. Daus and N. M. Ashkanasy, "The Case for the Ability-Based Model of Emotional Intelligence in Organizational Behaviour," *Journal of Organizational Behaviour* 26 (2005): 453–66.

4. This quote was attributed to Peter Drucker by Mark Fields of Ford Motor Company in 2006.

5. James Fischer, *Navigating the Growth Curve* (Boulder, CO: Growth Curve Press, 2006).

6. W. Chan Kim and Renée Mauborgne, *Blue Ocean Strategy: How to Create Uncontested Market Space and Make the Competition Irrelevant* (Cambridge, MA: Harvard Business Review Press, 2005).

7. Verne Harnish and the Team at Gazelles, *Scaling Up: How a Few Companies Make It . . . and Why the Rest Don't* (Ashburn, VA: Gazelles Inc., 2014).

8. Michael E. Porter, *Competitive Strategy: Techniques for Analyzing Industries and Competitors* (New York: Free Press, 1980).

9. W. Chan Kim and Reneé Maugorgne, *Blue Ocean Strategy* (Cambridge, MA: Harvard Business School Publishing Corporation, 2005).

10. Clayton M Christensen, *The Innovator's Dilemma* (Cambridge, MA: Harvard Business Review Press, 1997).

11. Nassim Nicholas Taleb, *Antifragile: Things That Gain from Disorder* (New York: Random House, 2012).

12. Simon Sinek, *Start with Why: How Great Leaders Inspire Everyone to Take Action* (London: Penguin Random House, 2009).

13. Jakki Mohr and Robert Spekman, "Characteristics of Partnership Success: Partnership Attributes, Communication Behavior, and Conflict Resolution Techniques," *Strategic Management Journal* 15, no. 2 (February 1994): 135–152; Jen C. Dyer, Julia Leventon, Lindsay C. Stringer, Andrew J. Dougill, Stephen Syampungani, Muleba Nshimbi, Francis Chama, and Ackson Kafwifwi, "Partnership Models for Climate Compatible Development: Experiences from Zambia," *Resources* 2, no. 1 (March 2013): 1–25.

STAGE 3

1. Charles Duhigg, *Smarter Faster Better: The Secrets of Being Productive in Life and Business* (New York: Random House, 2016).

2. Michael Michalko, *Thinkertoys: A Handbook for Creative-Thinking Techniques,* 2nd Edition. (Berkeley, CA: Ten Speed Press, 2006).

3. Adam Brandenburger, "Strategy Needs Creativity: An Analytic Framework Alone Won't Reinvent Your Business," *Harvard Business Review*, March–April 2019, 58–65

STAGE 5

1. Larry Bossidy and Ram Charan, *Execution: The Business of Getting Things Done* (New South Wales: Currency, 2002), 22.

2. Rob Cross and Andrew Parker, *The Hidden Power of Social Networks* (Cambridge, MA: Harvard Business Review Press, 2004).

3. Robert S. Kaplan and David P. Norton, "The Balanced Scorecard: Translating Strategy into Action," *Harvard Business Review*, January–February 1992, https://hbr.org/1992/01/the-balanced-scorecard-measures-that-drive-performance-2.

STAGE 6

1. Whit Mitchell, *Working in Sync: How Eleven Dartmouth Athletes Propelled Their College Sports Experience into Professional Excellence* (Eagle, ID: Aloha Publishing, 2013).

2. Andy Johnson, *Pushing Back Entropy: Moving Teams From Conflict to Health* (Eagle, ID: Restoration Publishing, 2014). In writing this book, Johnson incorporated several of Ron's models and practices and expanded upon them.

3. Mary Walton, *The Deming Management Method* (New York: Perigee Books, 1988).

4. Eliyahu Goldratt, *The Goal: A Process of Ongoing Improvement*, 30th Anniversary Edition (Great Barrington, MA: North River Press, 2014).

5. Douglas Stone and Sheila Heen, *Thanks for the Feedback: The Science and Art of Receiving Feedback Well* (New York: Viking Press, 2014).

6. Jeff Peters, *Agile Project Management* (self-pub., 2019).

STAGE 7

1. Richard Rumelt, *Good Strategy Bad Strategy: The Difference and Why It Matters* (London: Profile Books, 2017).

2. https://theleanstartup.com/principles

3. For more on idea management see, Baiya and Price, *The Innovator's Advantage: Revealing the Hidden Connection Between People and Process* (Eagle ID: Aloha Publishing, 2017).

4. F. R. David, *Strategic Management: A Competitive Advantage Approach*, 14th Edition. (New York: Pearson, 2013).

GLOSSARY

Enablers: The strategic themes that support the pillars (e.g., financial resources).

Key performance indicators (KPIs): A set of measures that will indicate whether an organization is achieving the key results.

Key results: Detailed descriptions of what an organization is trying to accomplish or how it will recognize superior performance. These are often made up of outputs, or intermediary measures, outcomes that create specific value for beneficiaries and impacts on society.

Lagging indicators: Measures that have already taken place.

Leading indicators: Measures that predict what will happen in the future.

Mission: The key business of organization that accomplishes its purpose, defined from the customer's perspective.

Objectives: More detailed descriptions of how an organization will achieve each of its goals, which describe how the organization will achieve its vision. We recommend three to five key objectives under each strategic goal.

Pillars: Strategic themes that directly drive the results desired by the organization.

Purpose: The reason why an organization exists, defining organizational identity and guiding the organization's development over time.

Scenario or contingency planning: Identifying and planning reactions to potential scenarios that may demand a significant change in the way the organization runs its business.

SLOC analysis: A summary of the organization's internal strengths and limitations, as well as the external opportunities and challenges that exist or may exist in the immediate future.

Strategic goals: Broad statements about what an organization wants to accomplish within the medium-term planning horizon. We recommend one or two goals under each strategic theme.

Strategic intelligence: The richness of awareness an organization has by understanding its current circumstances, systems, and energy, as well as by understanding the marketplace in which it operates, its current reputation in that marketplace, and the potential for strategic partnerships outside the organization itself.

Strategic options: A large number of possible pathways that can be pursued and that are created as a result of strategic intelligence and creative thinking.

Strategic themes: The strategic focus areas that are derived from a review and debate of strategic options. These themes will guide the organization's planning of goals, objectives, key results, tactics, and allocation of resources into a comprehensive strategic plan. Strategic themes should always have a direct connection to purpose, mission, and vision.

Strategy: The primary focus of an organization, which includes definitions of success, including the why, what, who, how, when, and where.

Tactics: A group of activities or tasks identified that are intended to achieve the objectives.

Tools: The models, frameworks, systems, and procedures that can be used to effectively execute the various strategy processes.

Values: The principles and standards that guide organizational behaviors and decisions.

Vision: How an organization wants to be perceived in the future; an expression of a desired end state and a dream of this future state in time. It represents what success will look like in 10 to 20 years.

INDEX

Figures and tables are indicated by an italicized *f* or *t* following a page number.

Seation, 101–59

effective communication of plan,
164–71, 165f
evaluating and adjusting use of
strategic intelligence, 176–77
integrating plan into daily workflows,
171–72
key processes of, 163, 163f
maintaining focus over time, 173–76
rhythms of focus and accountability,
172–73
strategic evaluation and learning,
187–88
strategic intelligence (stage 2), xviiif,
59–100
communication, 171
defined, 212
emotional intelligence vs., 59
evaluating and adjusting use of,
176–77
external environment assessments,
73–93
internal environment assessments,
60–73
SLOC analysis, 95–97
stakeholder analysis, 93–95
strategic evaluation and learning, 185
strategic options
defined, 206
evaluating and prioritizing, 121–28
generating, 109–15
tactical options vs., 129–30, 129f
strategic partnerships, 88–93
dormant partnerships, 91
leveraged partnerships, 91–92
missional partnerships, 92
partnership grid, 89–90, 90f
synergistic partnerships, 92–93
strategic planning for execution (stage
5), xviiif, 137–59
assigning roles and responsibilities,
144, 145t, 146–47
contingency planning, 138–40
key processes of, 138, 138f
key results, 140–42, 141f, 143t–44t
KPIs, 140, 142–43, 143t–44t
monitoring and evaluation, 154,
155t–56t, 157

scorecards, 147, 148t, 149, 150t–52t,
153
strategic evaluation and learning, 187
strategic themes, 106–7, 119–25, 119f
ABCD prioritization method, 121–23
communicating, 98, 164–67, 165f
creating, 120
defined, 206
enablers, 164–66, 165f, 205
goals and objectives, 131
key results and KPIs, 143t–45t
monthly meetings, 173, 176
pillars, 164–66, 165f, 211
resource–return grid, 123–25
scorecards, 148t, 150t–51t, 153
strategic and tactical options, 129–30
strategic thinking. See creative strategic
thinking
strategy
aligning talent and skills with, 19–23
anticipation, 9–10
becoming world-class strategist,
23–24
building aligned culture, 15–19
communication and, xviii
creating resilient, 9–15
criteria for good strategy, 193
defined, 206
external assessment, 10–11
fallacy that environments are
predictable, 2–3
fallacy that strategy is only about
vision and inspiration for the
future, 2–3
importance of, xvii
internal assessment, 12–15
organization's vs. individual's
aspirations, xvii
partnerships and, xvii
reasons for resistance to and
minimization of, 1
stages, xvii–xix, xviiif, 23–24
in VUCA environment, 2–3, 8
strategy creation, 101–59
creative strategic thinking, 103–17
skills needed for, 101
strategic decision-making, 119–36

ABOUT THE AUTHORS

Timothy Mwololo Waema is a professor of information systems in the School of Computing and Informatics at the University of Nairobi and founder-director of several start-up companies. He holds a PhD in strategic management of information systems from the University of Cambridge and a bachelor's honors degree in electrical and electronics engineering from the University of Bath. He has worked for many years as a researcher and practitioner at the intersection of information technology, strategy, policy, and innovation.

Over the last 20 years, Waema has facilitated more than 70 organizations, in both the public and the private sector, to develop or evaluate their medium-term strategy. He has also edited several books on IT and development.

Ron Price is an internationally recognized business advisor, executive coach, speaker, and author. Known for his creative and systematic thinking, business versatility, and practical optimism, Ron has worked in 15 countries and served in almost every level of executive management for more than

45 years. As the former president of a multimillion-dollar international company, Ron works shoulder to shoulder with executive leadership teams to bring strategic clarity and transformational results. In 2004, Ron founded Price Associates, a global leadership advisory firm. He is the author of nine books about business and personal growth. His previous books include *Treasure Inside: 23 Unexpected Principles That Activate Greatness, The Complete Leader: Everything You Need to Become a High-Performing Leader, The Innovator's Advantage: Revealing the Hidden Connection Between People and Process,* and *Growing Influence: A Story of How to Lead with Character, Expertise, and Impact.*

Evans Baiya is a scientist, consultant, author, and speaker. He has tackled innovation and strategy from all angles—as a research chemist, process development engineer, executive in multiple start-ups, global leader of research and development efforts in multiple countries, intellectual property portfolio manager at a global corporation, and policy advisor on research and commercialization. He works with a number of start-ups, large companies, academic institutions, and governments on strategy and planning, new product development, process improvements, R&D and innovation programs, technology transfer, and commercialization. He is the coauthor of *The Innovator's Advantage: Revealing the Hidden Connection between People and Process* with Ron Price.